PEMAQUID POINT
LIGHTHOUSE

PEMAQUID POINT LIGHTHOUSE

TRUDY IRENE SCEE

Published by The History Press
Charleston, SC
www.historypress.com

Copyright © 2020 by Trudy Irene Scee
All rights reserved

First published 2020

Manufactured in the United States

ISBN 9781467142243

Library of Congress Control Number: 2020930484

Notice: The information in this book is true and complete to the best of our knowledge. It is offered without guarantee on the part of the author or The History Press. The author and The History Press disclaim all liability in connection with the use of this book.

All rights reserved. No part of this book may be reproduced or transmitted in any form whatsoever without prior written permission from the publisher except in the case of brief quotations embodied in critical articles and reviews.

For my big brother,

Ron Holland,

our "Bub,"

with gratitude and love.

CONTENTS

Preface 9
Introduction 15

1. Pemaquid Point's Place in the Seascape of New England
    and Maine Lighthouses 21
2. The Pemaquid Point Lighthouse:
    The Early Decades Before Automation 43
3. The Lightkeepers of Pemaquid 61
4. Shipwrecks and Other Disasters 87
5. Pemaquid Point Lighthouse: Its Physical Structure, Personnel
    and Events After Automation 119

Conclusion 141
Appendix: Pemaquid Point Lighthouse Keepers 143
Notes 145
Bibliography 153
About the Author 157

PREFACE

When I was a very little girl, one of my favorite possessions was a whale bank my brother gave me. He brought it to me from Maine, some magical place where there was an ocean that had huge waves and stretched out forever, and whales and some mysterious but kind people named Aunt Dot and Uncle Ernie. He had lived there for many years, this older brother of mine, near a place called Old Orchard Beach. (Did it have apples? Peaches? Did the orchard still have lots of fruit? Did Aunt Dot have trees? How old was the orchard? Was it on a beach? Did Uncle Ernie play marbles? All these questions ran through my inquiring mind.)

My brother brought me this wonderful whale bank from one of his visits to his second home. It was ceramic, mostly blacks and grays with a hint of blue and some pink where the whale had his mouth partially open. He seemed to be smiling at me, this mystical creature. His tail was lifted up high. And he had a blowhole! What! What kind of creature was this that could toss grown people through the air when he pushed water out from a hole on his head? At least, someone said he could—probably my brother. But I learned to read very early, so maybe one of my books from the library was about whales. Maybe it had a drawing of a whale tossing a man into the air. I do not know. I only remember the image in my head.

I was a bit of a wild child when I was little, living in a small government apartment in way, way upstate New York. I loved the outside and the river nearby. But I wanted to see the place where horses ran free, where covered wagons crossed miles and miles of open land, and I wanted to see that magical place with the ocean.

Preface

So, when I was just turned five, or was maybe still four, we went there. My mom had someone's car, and we went to Maine. Maybe we went to pick up my brother. Probably we did. And we went to that old orchard place, and I don't remember being rewarded with trees or fruit or whales, but I did get to go on a few park rides—a little boat and a horse carousel ride. I remember those two rides. A boat and a horse!

And I saw *it* while my sister Juanita was off to the side yelling that something had just bit her, I saw *the ocean*. No doubt, I had seen it several minutes earlier. I have no memory of getting out of the car and walking down to the beach; I don't even know what beach it was, maybe Old Orchard Beach but maybe not. I only remember starring at it. I remember hearing the commotion—my sister thought a lobster had bit her—and just looking out. Looking out into the sea—the thing that had the same name as me, though spelled a bit different. (Scee is pronounced *sea*.) I was a child who could block out the world and focus on just that thing that captivated her. And the sea captivated me.

We left soon after that. It was only a quick trip to Maine. My mother was a first-class traveler even in those days when we didn't own a car, and she had crisscrossed the nation a number of times as a young woman.

I don't know what I thought standing beside the ocean that day. But I know the type of kid I was, and no doubt, I promised the ocean that I would return to see her. The whale bank I had was a he, but the ocean was a she. That's just the way it was. And I knew that someday I would return to her. And I found out, after the manuscript was in the editing phase, that I had already been to Maine at ages about one and three. I had wanted to go "home," and I had already been more than once.

And return to her I did. When I had a little girl of my own—just four years old and about to turn five—I returned. I came to Maine to live and go to graduate school, and I stayed.

And I looked. My daughter and I would get into the car most weekends and drive to the ocean. I didn't take maps; I would just drive. So, we ended up at some places many times and others just once or twice. I went until I found the place—not the place where I stood looking out to the sea as a little girl but the place that gave me the same feeling, the feeling of being on the edge of the world, of being in a wild place with the wind blowing and untold possibilities ahead. My daughter and my family know the place.

My brother, meanwhile, had moved to Kentucky and had become a rather high-ranking government official. One day he called me and told me that he had rented a house at Pemaquid Point for a week, and did we want to

Preface

Pemaquid Point Lighthouse at the turn of the twentieth century during the author's trip with her brother. The lighthouse and the property remained largely as they were in the late 1890s. *Photo by Trudy Irene Scee.*

visit overnight? Of course, we did. We brought Silly Sally Sue, our dog from Montana, where we lived before Maine. (Yes, I also made it to that place where horses run free and the prairies stretched out for miles.)

Sally was a bit of a problem, as they did not want dogs in the rental, but she was a good dog. On the night we arrived, my brother wanted to go for a walk late at night. A storm was about to break, so Sally and my daughter, Mariah, stayed with his friend and soon-to-be wife at the house while my brother and I went for a walk. We walked down a side road for a bit and then down another little road, and there it was: Pemaquid Point Lighthouse. The light was flashing through the darkness. We climbed around on those rocks—probably too far out, as I later learned—and then we walked up to the light. I was enchanted. I loved it. The waves were crashing, the wind was blowing and then the rain started. And come to find out, this wasn't my brother's first trip to Pemaquid Point. He may have gone there as a little boy with Aunt Dot and Uncle Ernie, and he had definitely been there as an adult. Why was this first time I was hearing about it?

At any rate, the storm hit. We walked back faster than we had come and discovered Sally hiding in the bathtub. She was a rescue dog and was afraid of loud noises, and the thunder was very loud.

About two years later, my brother called and said that he had rented the house again but could not come to Maine. Did we want the house for the week? Of course, we did. Mariah set up her space in an artist's loft room, and I chose a little room with a window seat. Mariah was, and is, an artist, and I am still a dreamer as well as a writer. I loved looking out over the bay from my window seat. We could hear the foghorn most mornings and see fishermen coming up in the evenings.

My brother came back to Maine to help me after I bought a house. It is a tiny house and still needed lots of work. So, he came a few times. The last time my brother came to Maine, we started to build a shed. And then, all of a sudden, he was calling out to me. He needed help.

I went over to where he was sitting on a bench facing the Penobscot River (the reason I chose that little house was the river that ran by it) and said he was dizzy and seeing lights. This had happened once before, and he said he just needed help getting back to the house.

I helped him get up. We took one step with him leaning on me for support. And then he fell. I could not stop him. He is still much bigger than me. He landed on me, and as I scooted out terrified, I saw his eyes roll back into his head. I thought he was dead. I ran next door for help—one of my neighbors is a nurse anesthetist. He was not home, but his partner called an ambulance, and I ran back and found my brother off the ground, walking in circles. I helped him back to the house.

My brother refused to go to the hospital. Over the next few days, he had terrible chills and mood swings and was often seemingly confused. It took more than six months, but he was finally diagnosed with Wegener's granulomatosis (GPA), an often-fatal autoimmune disorder. Before the last few years, it was always fatal. Relatively few people even know what it is.

My brother has suffered some debilitating effects from Wegener's. He cannot walk very far, and he certainly cannot climb out on the rocks at Pemaquid Point again. He will probably never be able to come to Maine again. He will probably never see the ocean again. That magical place, Pemaquid Point, is probably not in his future. I tried to take him to

Preface

Pemaquid the last time he visited, but he would not go. I think he knew it would be his last time here, and he wanted me to have a safe home. I wish he had gone, but I understand.

I have been back to that lighthouse many times and have climbed out on those rocks—a bit more carefully—many times. And this book is for Bub, also known as Ron Holland, with all the love and gratitude this little sister has for you. I know my sisters and mother and my daughter hold you dear too, as do many others, including Jono and Josh, your grandchildren, the cousins and your friends. I hope you like the book. And part of me still hopes that we can go to the ocean together again.

I RECENTLY FOUND A whale bank that is almost identical to the one my brother brought me when I was four. I found it at an antique store in Maine. It is on the shelves my brother built for me. And, by the way, I was a little miser with my pennies and nickels once I had them in my first whale bank all those years ago.

INTRODUCTION

Situated on the tip of Pemaquid Point in the town of Bristol, Maine, the Pemaquid Point Lighthouse attracts more than one hundred thousand visitors each year. As it is located on exposed bedrock, it offers a sweeping view of cascading rock down to the sea below. It is unique on the Maine coast, and its rocks are dangerous for those who attempt to walk them in ice or storms and for passing ships and boats. Rogue waves have swept people off the rocks even on "good" days, and storms have claimed the lives of more than one mariner—many, many more than one.

Pemaquid Point is a mysterious and beautiful place. But is has taken numerous lives over the centuries. It started doing so long before the United States became a nation and long before there were any aids to navigation in the area. Eventually, in the early 1800s, recognizing the dangers inherent in the point, the United States government established a lighthouse at Pemaquid.

Pemaquid Point itself is about three miles long, an example of Maine's many "fingers" of land projecting into the Atlantic Ocean. It has been deemed by some as the longest finger of the Maine coast. The ridge along its center slopes down in almost all directions to rocks and water. Islands are located off its coast—the closest, larger one being Monhegan Island. Spruce and fir cover parts of the rugged peninsula sometimes seemingly against the laws of nature. As early as the 1600s, Captain John Smith, when exploring the coastal area, questioned how the trees could grow on such inhospitable land and islands.

Introduction

Pemaquid Point Lighthouse in the late 1990s, as seen from the rocks below. *Photo by Trudy Irene Scee.*

Pemaquid Point actually has two "points" that project into the ocean at the end of the peninsula. The more northerly or easterly one has a much higher elevation than the westerly or southern one. The terms east and west may be more useful than north and south here, due to the unique landscape of coastal Maine. In this region, one gains more latitude than longitude, generally, over a limited distance. Between the two points at Pemaquid is a small cove or a somewhat more protected area than at the two points, yet it too has seen fatalities. When it came time to choose a location for a navigation aid, specifically a lighthouse, the higher, more rugged eastern promenade was chosen as it seemingly had fewer trees at the time, and it would be more visible to mariners from most angles. Some people, however, would later argue that the chosen site was actually not the better option.

Introduction

Commissioned in 1826 by John Quincy Adams, the original tower at Pemaquid sat seventy-nine feet above the sea at the entrance to Johns Bay and to Muscongus Bay on the easterly point of the peninsula. It was constructed of rubble stone. However, poor workmanship, particularly the use of saltwater in the mortar, caused the tower to deteriorate. In 1835, the current tower replaced it. The white tower, as built in 1835, measures thirty feet in height, sixteen feet in diameter at the base and ten feet in diameter at the top. An iron spiral staircase leads up to the light itself, which is seventy-nine feet above sea level. A lightkeeper's house was added to the grounds in 1837.

The rock on which the light tower rests is largely gray granite formed from volcanic activity, with bits of mica, feldspar and quartz included. The point is composed of rock compressed over millions of years and shaped by the sea into unique ridges or layers of rock, striped layers marked by various minerals and rock formations. Both metamorphic and igneous rock form the ledges and other formations—many twisted onto their sides with the passing of the millennia. One formation, it has been said, resembles the face of an older man.

At the point spreading out below the lighthouse, the igneous rock—generally white and seen especially on the long granite ridge leading down from the bell tower toward the ocean—formed when molten rock filled in fractures in the other rock formations and cooled slowly. Gneiss—a type of metamorphic rock formed by high pressures and temperatures—is found on sides of the granite layers, or rather, the layers are the gneiss formation of the rectangular boulders, some of them immense in size. Other rock formations jut up in a more usual manner—all of them dangerous to boats that get too close and people who get too careless. Waves crashing over the rocks can endanger those who think they are safe. And in some places, there is an undertow.

The Pemaquid Point Lighthouse has warned mariners of the rocks protruding into the sea for generations. It has, no doubt, saved many from shipwreck, though one can never know how many mariners turned away from danger. A light alone could not prevent all accidents; the Maine coast and the ocean are simply too perilous, especially in centuries gone by, when there were more shipping vessels on the sea and fewer aids to navigation. But even when disaster did occur, the lightkeeper was there to aid survivors in any way he (or, in other places, *she*) could in the nineteenth and early twentieth centuries, until automation reached the lighthouse in 1934. Five years later, the United States Coast Guard

Introduction

assumed control of both the light and emergency operations. Even with automation, though, the light remains compelling, even mysterious, with its aura of both security and danger. Its history is rich even if it still holds many secrets. And Pemaquid Point remains dangerous even as it proves enticing for so many visitors.

PEMAQUID LIGHT
OR
THE LIGHT

Hattie Vose Hall (1866–1942)
From Songs of the Coast of Maine, *Augusta, Maine, 1931*

I am the Lighthouse, holding
Nightly my torch on high;
Under me surge the waters,
Over me bends the sky.

Year after year I stand here
Holding my steady light,
Sending its ray of comfort
Into the darkest night.

Many a man has served me,
Tending the Light with care,
Many a vanished footstep
Passed up my winding stair.

Years pass and men pass with them,
Never my light grows dim,
One hands the torch to another,
Others will follow him.

So are the centuries moving,
Still serving men am I,
Constant through gales of winter
Calm beneath summer's sky.

Lights are the hope of the seaman,
Warning of rock and shoal,
We are the danger stations,
We are the sea-Patrol!

1

PEMAQUID POINT'S PLACE IN THE SEASCAPE OF NEW ENGLAND AND MAINE LIGHTHOUSES

Maine is at the top of New England—the most easterly part of the continental United States and the most northerly part of the East Coast—and early in America's history, the majority of the nation's lighthouses were located in New England. As late as 1825, almost two-thirds of America's lighthouses were located between Lubec, Maine, and New York City—a distance spanning about six hundred miles of the United States coastline. New England ruled the shipping industry during this era, and the region has a generally rocky coastline with an abundance of harbors, islands and shoals. New England needed its lighthouses, and it made that need well known. New England citizens and business leaders demanded lighthouses, and in the early 1800s, lights were largely a matter of supply and demand.[1]

Maine was critical in trade, made its demands known and received a number of lights during the late 1700s to mid-1800s. Pemaquid Point, like several other coastal locations, needed a light, but getting that light approved and constructed would take time. When built, however, it would prove a gem of light—one that, with others nearby, would come to illuminate the central Maine coast.

Lighthouses were built to save ships, and especially cargo, as much as they were to preserve human life during the early years. Fixed lights helped mariners know where they were and what dangers they should avoid, as well as which way they should aim their vessels for safety or to reach a given harbor. Fixed lights—as opposed to the open fires that were used at times—also helped ship masters avoid the "mooncussers" who tried to lure the ships to dangerous water, where their cargo could be looted, often at the expense of the boat and its crew. Anyone could build a bonfire on a cliff or open area to confuse mariners who sought a specific place. A lighthouse could make navigators fairly certain they were not being, literally, misled. Ships and their trade tended to go to the safest ports and thus most benefited those local communities.

Lighthouses played an extremely important role in the dead of night and in storms, but even on calm days, they provided visual markers to mariners. Distinctive shapes, sizes and colorings helped identify a particular station, and a boat's specific location.

The Boston Light, constructed in 1716 on Little Brewster Island in the Boston Harbor and lighted initially with tallow candles, was the first official lighthouse in the American colonies, and one of only seventy known in the world. Prior to this, in the Boston area as in some other locations, bonfires or burning barrels of pitch—lit when a vessel was spotted approaching—were used in high coastal areas to guide ships into port. In some instances, however, the aforementioned mooncussers lured boats to nearby locations to loot them. In response to this occurrence in the Boston area, and for other reasons, merchants petitioned the British in 1713, asking that a lighthouse be built, and they won their objective.

In 1719, the third keeper of the Boston Light (the first two keepers had drowned) started to use a canon to alert ships of their location and dangers in foggy weather because in dense fog, lighthouses and their beacons are often not visible. The keeper would fire the canon, wait for a response from a ship and then fire a return signal. Sound could, however, be deceptive, especially in foggy weather. The third keeper also recommended that a galley or walkway be constructed around the lantern room to allow for cleaning and removing snow and ice from the outside of the tower, and most freestanding lighthouses were subsequently built with galleys. During the Revolutionary War, colonists purposely destroyed their beloved Boston Light, as it was in the hands of British soldiers. In the 1780s, however, the new nation built a new light in the same location—one with a seventy-five-foot tower. It remains in place today.

During the colonial era, the colonists saw just eleven lighthouses built along the coast. Nine of these were located between what would become New London, Connecticut and Portland, Maine. The new country added fourteen more lights between the end of the Revolutionary War and 1799, according to Francis Ross Holland Jr. in his 1972 *American Lighthouses: Their Illustrated History Since 1716*. Ten of these new lighthouses were located north of New York City. The United States built another twenty-six lighthouses between 1800 and 1820, with the majority in the northeast.

In 1789, under the newly reorganized federal government with its new constitution replacing the nation's Articles of Confederation, the country had all lighthouses turned over to the federal government. All states surrendered jurisdiction over their lighthouses, as well as any lights then under construction. This involved one Maine light, the Portland Head Light.

After 1789, lighthouses were deemed part of the nation's shipping and commerce interests and would be overseen by the Department of Treasury for the next one hundred years and more, although they would undergo some transitions in management. The first secretary of the treasury, Alexander Hamilton, personally oversaw the lights for a few years and then turned that duty over to the commissioner of revenue. Supervision would pass back and forth between the two offices until 1820, at which time lighthouses fell under the supervision of the fifth auditor of the Department of Treasury, Stephen Pleasonton, whose management would prove controversial. He often worked with Winslow Lewis, a sea captain and engineer, not always to the best result. However, lighthouse construction did proceed, and general lighthouse oversight usually fell to the local collectors of custom, who would also be designated as superintendents of lighthouses.[2] Changes in lighting apparatus would prove crucial.

The earliest lighthouse built to serve the regions of Maine and New Hampshire—Maine being part of Massachusetts until 1820, while New Hampshire became an independent state in 1776—was the Portsmouth Harbor Light, first built in 1771 in what is now officially New Hampshire, though it is located between the two states on Great Island at the entrance of the Piscataquis River. The original lighthouse had a wooden tower that soon deteriorated and was replaced with another wooden one around 1804. This one had a granite foundation. In 1877 and 1878, the Lighthouse Board, then the governing body for American lights, erected an iron tower nearby to replace the wooden one. This 1878 tower remains in use.

In 1791, in Maine proper, before it became an independent state, work on the Portland Head Lighthouse was completed on Cape Elizabeth at the entrance to the Portland Harbor. It was the first lighthouse built under the new federal government; the second was built at the Chesapeake Bay the following year. The Maine light would undergo much modification in following years and decades, and several lights would be constructed nearby. The Portland Head Lighthouse with its tall, white, conical rubblestone tower remains one of Maine's most popular lights. It saw a

Pemaquid Point Lighthouse

Portland Head Light on Cape Elizabeth in the late 1990s. Its tower is taller than Pemaquid and was built decades before. *Photo by Trudy Irene Scee.*

number of tragedies over the years, as well as a major reconstruction like most of the early lighthouses.

By late 1795, the light at Sequin Island, commissioned by President George Washington and located about twenty-five miles east or northeast of Portland and about two and a half miles from the mouth of the Kennebec River, became operational. This was much closer to Pemaquid Point than any other light yet in existence, and at least one mariner would disastrously mistake the two in a storm a century later.

Lighthouse construction continued in Maine after the turn of the century. In 1807, the Franklin Island Lighthouse opened at Muscongus Bay, Maine, as did Whitehead Island Light at the entrance to the Penobscot Bay, as part of a contemporary push to protect harbors and bays. Maine's West Quoddy

Lighthouse—now noted for its distinctive horizontal red and white stripes—was added during the same era, in 1808. The light at West Quoddy would be located at essentially the most easterly tip of the nation. In 1820, it would secure the nation's first navigational fog bell.

In 1817 the Petit Manan Light was constructed off the coast of Steuben about fourteen miles from Bar Harbor. It was later deemed too short to be a first-class light, and in 1855, a new tower was constructed at the site, raising the beam to some 123 feet above sea level.

It was during the following decade, the 1820s, that Pemaquid Point Lighthouse was constructed at the entrance of Johns Bay to guide mariners at Muscongus Bay. The construction took place in a "flurry," under the new general superintendent of lights, Stephen Pleasonton, who, as noted, would prove a rather controversial figure. Pleasonton gained his position as superintendent of lighthouses in 1820, when Congress abolished the office of the commissioner of revenue and gave its duties to the fifth auditor of the treasury—a position Pleasonton served that year, the same year Maine became an independent state. From 70 American lighthouses in 1822, the number grew to 256 by 1843. A large share of these were in New England and a number of them were in Maine. A corresponding growth also occurred in lightships.[3]

West Quoddy Lighthouse in winter. The lighthouse is the most easterly and northerly one located on land in Maine. *Photo by Trudy Irene Scee.*

Pemaquid Point Lighthouse

Another view of the light at West Quoddy. Its distinctive red and white stripes serve as an aid to Mariners in the daytime. *Photo by Trudy Irene Scee.*

An angled view of the tower and the keeper's house at Pemaquid Point. *Photo by Trudy Irene Scee.*

Between 1821 and 1825, at least twenty-three lighthouses were built in America. Pemaquid Point lighthouse went into operation in 1827, while nearby at Boothbay Harbor, the Burnt Island Light was operational in 1821. Mariners would fatally mistake this light in later years while actually located off the coast of Pemaquid Point.

Elsewhere, the Maine coast saw the construction of Libby Island Light (1822) at the entrance of Machias Bay, Owl's Head (1826) at Rockland Harbor and Dice Head (1829) at the entrance to the Penobscot Bay. These were part of a national commitment to guard America's bays, harbors and rivers, while others were built to serve more than "local" traffic, in other words, to reach beyond the harbors and bays of Maine and elsewhere.

Pemaquid Point Lighthouse

Left: The Prospect Harbor Lighthouse in the 2010s. The lighthouse is no longer accessible to the public. *Photo by Trudy Irene Scee.*

Opposite: Rockland Breakwater Lighthouse. The seawall leading to the light is close to a mile long. *Photo by Trudy Irene Scee.*

Those Maine lights built to reach farther out to sea included the Isles of Shoals Light on the border between Maine and New Hampshire (built in 1821 and rebuilt in 1857); in Maine proper, the Monhegan Island Light (constructed in 1824 and updated in 1857); Moose Peak Station on Mistake Island (constructed in 1827 and rebuilt in 1887); and the two towers erected at Matinicus Rock in 1827.[4]

In 1848, the original towers at Matinicus Rock were replaced with granite ones, and the northern tower was essentially dismantled in 1924, when the federal government determined that all light stations should have only a single beacon. A second tower remains, but it has no lantern room or beacon. Other stations would be constructed in Maine and the rest of the country with multiple towers, and these would see similar changes.

In 1828, just after construction of the towers at Matinicus Rock, the Cape Elizabeth Light—the light station also known as Two Lights—went into operation. It had twin towers and was established to guard the southwestern entrance to Casco Bay not far from Portland Harbor. The second light,

Pemaquid Point Lighthouse

Pemaquid Point Lighthouse

Above: The Cape Elizabeth Lighthouse. Once again, the white tower set against the red roofs serves as an aid to mariners in daylight hours. *Photo by Trudy Irene Scee.*

Left: The tower at Cape Elizabeth is one of Maine's tallest land lights. *Photo by Trudy Irene Scee.*

Pemaquid Point Lighthouse

Classic Maine rock formations at Seal Cove, not unlike those at Pemaquid Point. *Photo by Trudy Irene Scee.*

located quite close to the first one, was deactivated in 1924, as was one of the lights at Matinicus. Before then, in 1874, the original rubblestone towers, located some 900 feet apart, were replaced with twin conical cast-iron towers. The deactivated tower is now privately owned, as is the land surrounding the current, in-use tower. It is 67 feet tall, and sitting on a high point like the Pemaquid Light, it has a focal plane of 129 feet above the ocean. In 1970, it was the first lighthouse to appear on a U.S. postage stamp.

Also in 1828, the Baker Island Lighthouse went into operation near present-day Acadia National Park to guide mariners into Frenchman Bay. It would have a troubled early history. The first lightkeeper served for some time, but it seems there was some difficulty, and he was dismissed from his duties after twenty-one years. After this, his sons continually harassed the new lightkeeper, including denying him access to the island's only boat landing—his means to leaving the island, securing supplies and so forth. It took legal proceedings to settle the matter, which, in part, stemmed from an imprecise 1806 land transfer. The old keeper's family claimed that they owned the entire island.

Pemaquid Point Lighthouse

One of the lights at Two Light Lighthouse Station on Cape Elizabeth. This is the light that remains operational but is closed to the public. One can take photographs from the beach below, where a lightkeeper and his assistants rescued two men off a sinking schooner in the 1800s. *Photo by Trudy Irene Scee.*

The old deed at Baker Island was found defective, and the government compromised with the family in the 1850s by accepting nineteen acres of land and leaving the balance for the family. In 1855, a new light was built on Baker Island. The land ownership issue came up again in the 1890s, but no major changes could be made by then, except that the government did secure a clear right-of-way from the boat landing to the lighthouse property. A property issue would also arise at Pemaquid Point, and it may be that the prompt attention given it reflected the earlier events at Baker Island.[5]

In the meantime, in the same region, Mount Desert Rock Light, located about twenty-five miles south of Mount Desert Island, was added to the navigational guides in Maine in 1830. It was rebuilt in 1848 and again in 1857, when it was raised to sixty feet. Bear Island Light near Acadia National Park went into operation in 1839 and was rebuilt in 1890. Other lights were added in Maine during this time, such as the Saddleback Ledge Light at the outer eastern entrance to Penobscot Bay in 1839, featuring a large conical granite tower that survives to the current day.

While lighthouse construction continued, on April 16 and 17, 1851, a fatal storm hit New England. The iron Minots Ledge Light, located just

Pemaquid Point Lighthouse

south of Boston and put into operation only the year before, was destroyed when raging waves and wind ripped it free of its base, causing it to topple into the sea and taking two assistant lighthouse keepers to their deaths. The head lightkeeper was not at the lighthouse at the time. The first lightkeeper at Minots Ledge—who happened to be the first lightkeeper at Pemaquid Point as well—had urged that the tower be strengthened before the disaster occurred. His warnings had not been heeded, and he had resigned the post.[6]

Following the disaster, a lightship would be used in the Minots Ledge location until 1860, when a new tower went into operation. But the tragic 1851 event, as well as some problems with the lighting apparatuses in American lighthouses, caused the federal government to pause, review the lights and revise the oversight of the lights in Maine and the rest of the nation.

What happened in the 1850s represented a major redirection in American lighthouse administration and was, in part, due to the apparatuses used to power the beacons. Maine would not be exempt from the changes, just as its history had been tied to shared fuel sources, lamps and other factors in the past.

The main lights at Campobello Island just off the coast of northeastern Maine. The Canadian and American governments both have jurisdiction on the island. *Photo by Trudy Irene Scee.*

Early lamps, which had replaced candles and other lighting sources, might use sperm oil or others for fuel, but they also required wicks to be operational. In about 1790, lamps that were essentially a set or series of wicks protruding from a bowl of oil came into use. First used in Britain, they were called spider lamps and generally gave off fumes that would sting the eyes and nostrils of the lightkeepers. Overall, these produced more light than older ones, at least when properly installed. These were the main lamps used in the United States until 1812, when retired captain or shipmaster Winslow Lewis—who had some connection with the lighthouse service—started experimenting with a lamp developed by Ami Argand.

Argand invented a lamp with a hollow circular wick in 1781. The resulting flame burned brighter and more intensely than others, as oxygen passed along both the outside and the inside of the wick. It was generally smokeless, and the lamp and wicks were deemed as bright as seven candles or other wicks. Fifteen or more of these lamps might be used when a strong coastal beam was needed. England began using the lamps in 1789, as did France, and they used them with parabolic reflectors, coated with silver and placed behind the lamp to direct the light beam and increase the power.[7] Soon, another scientist, Augustus Fresnel, would modify Argand's hollow wick for use in his lenses and vastly improve the light as a navigational aid in Europe. Fresnel's innovations, however, would take some time to reach American lighthouses. In the meantime, the Argand lamp, or a variation thereof, would light America's beacons.

The Argand lamp with a parabolic reflector reached American lights in 1810, replacing the older spider lamps and the new system. Besides giving better results, it burned about half the oil as had the older spider lamps. However, retired sea captain and inventor or engineer Winslow Lewis soon made some changes to Argand's lamp and patented it himself. He persuaded the government to back his lamp, and it was installed in all new lights and replaced lamps in older lights.[8]

Changes also occurred concerning the fuels burned in the lamps over time, as well as in the actual lamps, which greatly increased the intensity or output of a lighthouse. Beginning in the seventeenth century, sperm whale oil replaced wood (up to thirty candles at once were also used) as the main fuel in America. Sperm oil was used at Pemaquid Point for some time, but by the mid-nineteenth century, whale populations had been depleted, and sperm oil was becoming increasingly expensive.[9]

Lard was used in some places beginning in about 1864, but it gave off black smoke that would quickly coat the inside of the lens, so another

Dice Head Lighthouse on Deer Island—one of the few island lights a visitor can drive to via a bridge from the mainland. *Photo by Trudy Irene Scee.*

option was sought. A few other fuels were tried and soon replaced for various reasons. In 1877, kerosene was introduced at many lights and became quite popular. Before this, in 1866, the Statue of Liberty was lit with electricity, making it a navigational aid in New York Harbor until 1902. It took until the 1940s for electricity to reach many lighthouses, so in the meantime, other fuel sources had to suffice. In Maine, kerosene remained important.

Sound also played a role in alerting vessels to danger in Maine. As noted, canons were used at the Boston Light and some other lights in the early years, followed by bells, which were in general use by about the late 1850s. After the Civil War, in the mid-1860s, horns began to replace bells.[10]

Until Augustin-Jean Fresnel (1788–1827), a French scientist, invented a new way to increase the visibility or intensity of the light through the use of prisms, American lights operated pretty much the same as those in Europe. However, the lamps developed by Lewis proved less effective overall than his model, the original Argand lamp with its truly parabolic reflector, thus the United States soon fell behind Europe in its technology.[11]

Before Fresnel, people had tried to increase the intensity of the navigational lights by using different fuels, placing mirrors behind the flame and using magnifying glass in front of the flame. Still, most lights could be seen for only a few miles, even in ideal weather conditions. In stormy weather, a light might be seen only a mile away. This was certainly better than no light but was not necessarily sufficient warning for all ships in treacherous locations.[12]

Fresnel developed a new lens in 1822 by bending the light and focusing it into a narrow beam, which greatly amplified the power of the light, such that it might be seen for close to twenty miles, depending on the exact light and the weather. Fresnel used prisms at the top and bottom of his lenses to achieve this amplification. The prisms bent essentially all of the light generated by the lamp flame so that it shone in the same direction. Before this, much of the light of the flame had been "wasted" as it shone in all directions. In addition, Fresnel used powerful magnifying glasses with his lenses.

Fresnel made seven orders, or sizes of lenses. The largest was the first order lens, which gave off the strongest beam and would be used to get the beacons far out to sea, as opposed to strictly harbor use. The smallest was the sixth order lens (there was one classed at an order of three and a half, hence the seeming number discrepancy), which was primarily used for harbor lights. Order was determined by the distance of the flame from the lens, or the focal distance. Fresnel died just five years after creating his revolutionary lens and did not secure a patent.

A first order Fresnel lens could be as large as six feet wide and twelve feet tall. Lights that served both harbors and the near ocean might have a fourth and fifth order lens. Only two first order lenses were installed in New England—one in Boston and the other at Sequin Island in Maine. Fresnel lenses could be used with different lamps and fuels, but they had to use the hollow concentric wicks. The wicks were placed one inside the other. Whale oil was used first, as it was with other types of lenses and lamps during this time.[13]

The United States had adopted Lewis's lamp only a decade before Fresnel developed his lens, one greatly superior to what had been used in the past. By the War of 1812, or soon thereafter, all but nine of the U.S. lights were fitted with Lewis's system. Lewis tried to increase their efficiency by placing a greenish-tinted lens in front of the lamp, but this did not increase their effect. After about twenty-five years, most of them were removed. Lewis maintained a relationship with the Lighthouse Service, especially through Stephen Pleasonton, then charged with the care of U.S. lights, and kept his system in place. However, there were numerous complaints that American

Pemaquid Point Lighthouse

Bass Harbor Lighthouse on Mount Desert Island. It is now maintained by Acadia National Park and is an island light accessible by car. *Photo by Trudy Irene Scee.*

lights were not up to par with European lights, and indeed, an 1838 investigation pointed out numerous problems. It was the Lewis system that would have been installed at Pemaquid Point in the 1820s.

The federal government finally sent Commodore Mathew C. Perry to Europe to examine lighthouses in 1838, while it investigated matters at home. Perry was authorized to purchase two Fresnel lenses to experiment with in the United States. He returned with a first order lens and a revolving second order lens. The lenses were installed, and even as they aged over the next decade and more, they were still deemed superior to the Lewis lamps, which Pleasonton continued to support. Change came only through congressional action.

Concerned about complaints regarding the effectiveness of American lights—from mariners, merchants and others—Congress authorized a board to investigate American lighthouses in 1851. It found U.S. lights to be inferior in quality, with the apparatuses lacking in several ways, some simply poorly constructed with substandard oil being used, inadequate ventilation provided and defective reflectors installed (most were spherical not parabolic as they were supposed to be). It noted other problems, including shoddy tower construction, towers too short to serve their purposes and poor management of the stations by often untrained lightkeepers. The American lights were inferior and outdated. And some of the lighthouses themselves had serious issues—not just the one at Minot's Ledge, which was swept away in 1851, causing the deaths of its assistant keepers.

Engineer I.W.P. Lewis (who happened to be Winslow Lewis's nephew) would lead the investigation into American lighthouses in Maine, as well as in New Hampshire and Massachusetts. He had quite a bit to say on the placement of buoys and the lack of diversity in the Maine lights, as well as on their power and their light intensity. His criticisms and recommendations led to changes in Maine, including at Pemaquid Point.

Soon after the various reports came in, Congress reorganized the U.S. Light Service, complete with a new board of directors or supervisors—mostly comprising the same men who had served on the investigative committee—and ordered that Fresnel lenses be installed in all new lighthouses and in all lighthouses in need of new lighting apparatuses. The board set out converting the lights to Fresnel lenses, and those lenses still remain in use in some places, including at Pemaquid Point. The lighthouses would need only one Fresnel lens each (some had to have multiple lenses before) but did need more than one wick. Eventually, electric bulbs would

Pemaquid Point Lighthouse

Left: Marshall Point Lighthouse is the closest land light to the northeast of Pemaquid Point and another very popular coastal light. *Photo by Trudy Irene Scee.*

Right: Another view of the Marshall Point Lighthouse. *Photo by Trudy Irene Scee.*

light the lenses, although recently, new lighthouses have been equipped with a different type of light altogether.

In 1852, the Bureau of Lighthouses replaced the Lighthouse Board and all previous services and divided the nation into twelve new lighthouse districts. The first district, which included Pemaquid Point, began at the St. Croix River in Maine. Each district had an inspector and was eventually appointed an engineer when the duties falling on the inspector became too demanding. Initially, it was arranged that each inspector was a naval officer and charged with supplies, salaries and so forth, while the engineer was an army officer charged with supervising the building of new lights and inspecting each light station every three months. Later, a depot would be added at each district headquarters.

Lighthouse construction continued, and a few more lights went up in Maine. In 1858, under new supervision at the federal level, the Bass Harbor Light, situated on Mount Desert Island, went into operation at the entrances to Bass Harbor and Blue Hill Bay. It remains in use, was

Pemaquid Point Lighthouse

The Spring Point Ledge Light connected with a walkable seawall to Cape Elizabeth. *Photo by Trudy Irene Scee.*

automated in 1974 and has recently come under the control of the contiguous Acadia National Park.

In 1897, the Spring Point Ledge Light was built on a newer breakwater at Portland Harbor. It was a prefabricated cast-iron "cone." The prefabrication style was selected in an attempt to reduce costs and to create an efficient type of light to use as a marker for underwater hazards, as well as to mark land. It is a caisson-style lighthouse, and purportedly, it is the only working one in the United States up to which one can walk. This style of light is generally used offshore (such as Maine's Lubec Channel Lighthouse, built in 1889–90) and not on land or breakwaters, and they typically have iron or concrete bases. They are often called "sparkplug" or "bug" lights.

Not to confuse the situation but to provide sufficient navigational aid, in 1855, not far away, the Lighthouse Service had already constructed a small wooden lighthouse at the end of an earlier breakwater. The breakwater was then extended farther into the bay, and in 1875, the site saw a new "tower" built—one made of iron, with its curved iron plates covered with Corinthian columns—on a granite base or caisson. The new Portland Breakwater or Bug Light was designed to resemble a Greek monument.

Pemaquid Point Lighthouse

A long view down the granite rocks at Pemaquid Point—the scene of more than one shipwreck, even after the lighthouse was added in 1827. *Photo by Trudy Irene Scee.*

Once the Spring Point Ledge Light came into existence, however, the keeper stationed there was charged with taking care of both it and the Portland Bug Light. The Bug Light station then lost its keepers house and other buildings. The Bug Light is no longer in service, as it was decommissioned in 1943, but it and Spring Point Ledge remain popular with visitors. Like those surrounding Pemaquid Point, a series of lighthouses was often needed to guide ships in dangerous waters, and those on Cape Elizabeth and other parts of the Portland Harbor did just that, although, even after their installation, not all wrecks and mishaps could be avoided.

In 1910, after the flurry of lighthouse construction and reconstruction, another change came to the lighthouse system. New districts were added, and the charge of them went to civilians. Within two years, all light districts were under the charge of civilians. However, in 1939, as part of the Presidential Reorganization Act, the Lighthouse Bureau was abolished and incorporated its services into the U.S. Coast Guard. Lighthouse personnel could either enter military service or keep their civilian status. These changes would affect the lives and duties of the lightkeepers and sometimes lead to even greater changes. By 1939, however, other important developments had occurred at Pemaquid Point, as elsewhere.

2

THE PEMAQUID POINT LIGHTHOUSE

THE EARLY DECADES BEFORE AUTOMATION

The Pemaquid region saw Caucasian visitors long before the construction of its lighthouse in the 1820s. It saw them long before America became a nation. The Pemaquid Point Lighthouse is located in Bristol, Maine, and immigrants from Bristol, England, established a settlement at Pemaquid in 1631. By 1607, however, there was evidence of a previous English settlement existing at Pemaquid Point a little farther up the peninsula. And long before then, First Peoples or Native Americans had a presence in the area.

Records exist of a visit by Captain George Waymouth and twenty-nine men of England aboard his ship *Angel Gabriel* in 1605, predating most settlements in the New World, including Jamestown. Waymouth sailed from England that March and first reached Monhegan Island off the coast of Pemaquid. He then visited various parts of the Maine coast, including the Pemaquid region. Numerous ships would reach the area in following years, and according to one record, between 1607 and 1622, "109 ships entered and cleared from the harbors of Pemaquid and its dependencies, where they did more or less business in the discharge and receipt of cargoes and commerce with Europe." Even ships tasked with taking settlers to Jamestown and Virginia found it worthwhile to return via the Pemaquid area to load up with fish and furs to sell in Europe. Pemaquid was already a busy fishing and trading center while settlers elsewhere were still struggling to establish colonies. By 1622, at least thirty ships regularly traded and fished in the Pemaquid region. Yet, as Europeans would learn, the region was dangerous, even without their hostilities with the First Peoples or Native Americans.[14]

Pemaquid Point Lighthouse

In 1625, John Brown of Bristol, England, made an agreement or land purchase at Pemaquid from the Native Peoples, called the Pemaquid Indians in subsequent years. It was signed by Natives Samoset and Unongoit. The deed is purportedly the first such land sale in New England and perhaps in America. A subsequent 1631 deed signed by English authorities, namely King Charles, without Native approval granted some twelve thousand acres at Pemaquid for settlement. Known as the "Patent," it truly opened the region for European settlement.

The name "Pemaquid" is thought to be Abenaki for, essentially, "situated far out." Other sources assert that it is a Micmac name, but the Micmac are generally deemed part of the Abenaki Confederation. The Native or First Peoples lived or spent parts of the year in the region long before European settlement and, in all probability, never intended to relinquish their interests and fishing grounds to the English or anyone else. Yet, the English and others continued to come to the region.

The town of Pemaquid eventually reached a population of about two hundred people and was incorporated as the town of Bristol in 1665, before the Abanaki burned much of it down during King Philip's War a decade later. The town, or what remained of it (although some settlers rebuilt), suffered subsequent violent interactions with native peoples and was abandoned by the white colonists sometime before 1700, before being reestablished in 1729. Fort William Henry was erected at Pemaquid in 1692 but was destroyed by New France in the Siege of Pemaquid in 1696. It had been the largest fort in New England, though it was still rather quickly invaded. In 1908, a reconstructed fort was built in the same place and remains a popular attraction in the twenty-first century.

Before the construction of the original fort, which may have provided a visual aid to navigation to some degree, especially during daylight, a ship met its demise at Pemaquid Point. This ship had traversed the Atlantic in the past, and the captain knew the nearby harbors. Still, the rocks brought destruction. As will be seen, during 1635, a shipwreck took human lives, livestock and property to their doom on the granite rocks that push into and up from the sea. Thus, early on, mariners learned the region could be a deadly one.

By 1729, New England had become fairly prosperous, and Pemaquid was a busy place. The need for some sort of permanent marker continued to be felt by the colonists. Maine as a whole—although it was not yet called Maine—had a dangerous coastline with frigidly cold water, rocky shores and seemingly endless islands and peninsulas and harbors to navigate.

Pemaquid Point Lighthouse

A postcard of the reconstructed Fort William Henry located near the Pemaquid Point Lighthouse. *Public Doman.*

Colonists wanted to see a light at Pemaquid Point, but it would take some time before they acquired one.

The Sequin Light, with its fifty-three-foot tower located two and a half miles out from the mouth of the Kennebec, and the Monhegan Light located across the waters from Pemaquid, with its forty-seven-foot tower, would be constructed before the Pemaquid Point light. These were constructed in 1795 and 1824 respectively. Pemaquid's time would finally come but not before some people in its vicinity witnessed a naval battle.

During the War of 1812, on September 5, 1813, a battle occurred off the coast of Pemaquid and was witnessed by many of the townspeople. The USS *Enterprise*, a sixteen-gun naval brig, sailed from the Kittery Naval Yard to cruise the Maine coast and offer American ships protection from British attacks. It engaged a British fourteen-gun brig, the *Boxer*, four miles south of Pemaquid Point on September 5, 1813. The *Enterprise* defeated the British ship at the cost of the lives of its captain and another man. Four of eleven men wounded on the American side would later expire. On the British side, the captain and fourteen men died during the gun battle, and another fourteen men sustained injuries.[15] Townspeople were hard pressed to determine the winner, however, as both vessels "limped" away from the battle.

With the danger at the important location of Pemaquid well known, and in an era of widespread lighthouse construction, President John Quincy Adams commissioned the light at Pemaquid, and the U.S. Congress appropriated $4,000 for the light's construction on March 2, 1827. Then, on June 29, 1827, Samuel and Sarah Martin sold a few acres of land to the federal government for $90. The Martins were descended from survivors of the 1635 wreck at Pemaquid Point and had used the land primarily to graze their sheep. With presidential approval, funding approved by Congress and the necessary land acquired, construction soon began.

Pemaquid Point Lighthouse

The superintendent of lighthouses for Maine at that time, Isaac Ilsley, contracted with Jeremiah Berry of Thomaston, a bricklayer by trade, "to build, finish, and complete a Lighthouse and Dwelling House at Pemaquid Point," according to the surviving agreement. Berry was to use undressed stone ("suitable split stone") and "good lime mortar" for the job and make the tower eighteen feet in diameter at its base and ten feet in diameter at its top. The material used is also known as rubblestone. The walls were to be three and a half feet thick and graduated uniformly to a two-foot thickness at the top. At the top, "an arch would be turned." On top of this, an eleven-and-a-half-foot-diameter soap stone disk that was five inches thick was to be erected, with a "scuttle" allowing for access to the glassed-in lantern or lamp room. There was also to be a "stair of hard pine, clear of sap, seasoned and planed, with an iron ladder at the top reaching into the 'scuttle,'" as quoted by Hilda Libby in her 1975 "Story of Pemaquid Lighthouse" pamphlet.[16]

The price to be paid to Berry, $2,800, was to include the keeper's dwelling. The contract specified that the keeper's house be built measuring thirty-four by twenty feet, with a chimney dividing its two rooms and a fireplace fronting each room and closets and shelves in "back of the chimney." The one-story stone structure, "eight feet at the clear," was to have eighteen-inch-thick stone walls and an attached ten-by-twelve-foot kitchen with its walls built to the same specifications as the rest of the dwelling. The kitchen would also have a chimney with "an iron crane, trammel and hooks; on one side an oven of middling size with an iron door, on the other side a sink with a gutter to lead through the wall, out of the house." The house may have had lofts for sleeping, as it was noted that stairs were to lead off to the chambers, which would be partitioned off. All of the rooms were to have lathed and plastered walls and double floors "well nailed." The house and kitchen were to be shingled with seasoned boards.[17]

Built and operational soon after the authority for it was granted, the original tower at Pemaquid had a light focal point seventy-nine feet above the sea at the entrances to Johns Bay and Muscongus Bay. Due to poor workmanship, however, it soon had to be replaced. In particular, the probable use of saltwater in the mortar may have caused the tower to deteriorate. The second contract issued for a new tower—under the auspices of the new superintendent of lighthouses in Maine, John Chandler—was close to the original one but specified that no saltwater could be used in mixing the mortar. Instead, "only the best lime mortar; the same to be used never to have been wet with saltwater; the mortar to be mixed with fresh water."[18]

The first contract also called for the best lime mortar, but apparently, the contractor had not used fresh water throughout. To further ensure that a solid and sturdy new tower was constructed, the contractor, this time a Joseph Berry, a mason from Georgetown, was to make the walls one layer of solid stone—"or where there is more than one thickness of stone, the walls are to be carried up solid and bound together, and not to be done by building two walls, and filling in [with mortar] in the middle," as apparently had been true under the first contractor. In addition, the new contract specified that "all of the stones are to be so laid that the upper side of the stone will not incline downward on the inside, and thereby tend to convey the water through the wall." Using existing materials for the most part, the contracted price for the new tower was $1,395. As built, four windows provided natural daylight inside the tower.[19]

After Berry completed the reconstruction, the first lightkeeper at Pemaquid, Isaac Dunham, added a note to the contract, stating, "Capt. Berry has completed the Light House in a good workman like manner and according to the Contract in every way—and I will vent[ure] to say, a Better Tower and Lantern never was built in this State. Also the Lamps, reflectors, and apparatus is according to Contract." Dunham wrote "Overseer" after his signature at the end of his note and would have reported to the Lighthouse Service that all had transpired as expected. Visibility of the light was about

A surviving note from Keeper Isaac Dunham attesting to the good work done by the contractor on the reconstruction of the tower. *Public Domain.*

two miles.[20] The tower as built in 1835 remains in use today, with crucial improvements having been made to the lighting apparatus to substantially enhance its reach.

Before the 1852 reorganization of Lighthouse Service, lighthouses were contracted out, often to the lowest bidder, and problems like those seen at Pemaquid were not uncommon, although some contractors did do excellent jobs. In 1838, however, an investigation would show that numerous lighthouses had been built of substandard materials (up to 40 percent were inferior in quality), and Pemaquid might have been so deemed had its initial construction not been so poor that it was replaced before the investigation. Problems with the lighting apparatuses were also identified during the inspections, but no changes were made for a number of years.

The lighthouse style at Pemaquid was one of two standard forms built during the era when Stephen Pleasonton had control of American lights. The basic tower in this style was conical—as seen at Pemaquid—or square, octagonal or pyramidal in shape. The towers in this type were generally built of fieldstone or rubblestone or of cut-stone, brick or wood. The keeper's house would be constructed separately, as at Pemaquid, although they might well be attached. The second style built during Pleasonton's era was a keeper's house, generally of one and a half stories, with a tower and light topping the house. Pleasonton adopted this form in a situation where insufficient money was secured to build a separate tower and house and subsequently used it in places where only a low beacon was required.[21]

The existing white tower at Pemaquid, as built in 1835, measures thirty feet in height above the ground, sixteen feet in diameter at the base and ten feet in diameter at the top. The light itself is forty-eight feet above the ground and seventy-nine feet above mean sea level. An advantageous position on the cliffs just above the long and rocky slope and point down to the sea made a greater height unnecessary, which, in turn, largely determined the diameter of the edifice at its base. The pine spiral staircase was later replaced with an iron one, and an iron-fenced galley surrounds the lantern room, which is iron framed and octagonal in shape.[22]

The lighthouse at Pemaquid would have been outfitted with Lewis lamps and reflectors—the type being installed in all new lighthouses during that time. They were based on the Ami Argand lamp and within thirty years would be deemed highly inferior to the lamps and apparatus being used in Europe. At that time, Pemaquid's would be replaced.

Records show that the lamps installed were indeed those developed by Winslow Lewis, as Isaac Illsley had signed a contract in 1827, the same day

Pemaquid Point Lighthouse

Pemaquid Point Lighthouse circa 1995. The tower is shown in good repair and without some of the signage added later. *Photo by Trudy Irene Scee.*

he signed the contract for the first tower at Pemaquid, with Lewis to have him "fit up the Light House at Pemaquid Point with ten patent lamps and ten, sixteen-inch reflectors." The total cost came to $500.[23]

The 1827 contract between Illsley and Lewis also noted that Lewis would supply "six double X tin butts, to hold ninety gallons each and painted three coats, and six wooden horses, two spare lamps, one lantern canister and iron trivet and double tin wick box and one glazier's diamond, one torch, one hand lantern and lamp, two pairs scissors, two files, two tube cleaners, one stove funnel, one oil feeder, and all other apparatus, in the same manner as Light-Houses have been fitted by said Lewis with the Addition of Black's apparatus for conducting the heat to the lamps to the oil therein."[24] Thus as discussed, the lighthouse adopted lamps, or rather a set of them plus all associated materials for maintaining them, which were obsolete before they were even installed, as Fresnel already developed his lens and system five years earlier.

However, Pemaquid Point may have gotten its way around some of the issues involved in maintaining the lights, especially during the cold winter months. Its first keeper, Isaac Dunham, was an inventive sort, and he developed a system to help prevent lamp oil from congealing in cold weather—a concern of every lightkeeper in New England. He patented his invention, and in 1837, the U.S. Congress authorized the Department of the Treasury to adopt his improvements. It is uncertain how widely his invention was adopted, but no doubt, it was used at Pemaquid Point to help with one of winter's most pressing concerns for those who had responsibility for lighting the Maine coast. Dunham would later become a keeper at Minot's Ledge Light in Massachusetts, and surely introduced his design there.[25]

With Pemaquid Point's second tower up and stable, its means of reaching the lamp secure and a lightkeeper's house at the ready, the mid-1830s on would see a relatively smooth operation during the balance of the century, except when disaster struck, and disaster would strike more than once. In the meantime, before it gained a new lighting apparatus and the worst disaster occurred, both a president of the United States and engineer I.P.W. Lewis would visit the lighthouse to ascertain its efficiency and quality and to meet its keeper.

I.P.W. Lewis visited Pemaquid Point in 1842, when it was under the care of its third keeper, Jeremiah S. Means. Lewis was making a survey of the regional lights at the time and praised what he found at Pemaquid. He reported that "the general state of the tower [is] good," as was that of the keeper's house. The tower was proving leaky in storms though. Lewis also noted that eleven panes of glass in the lantern, which held ten lamps and their reflectors, were broken.[26] His report on the region as a whole, however, would not be as positive.

In December 1846, James K. Polk came to Pemaquid Point. He stayed overnight at the Damariscotta House on December 26, listing his residence as Tennessee instead of Washington, D.C., where he was then residing as America's eleventh president. He was in the area to look at the light at Pemaquid Point. Presidential signatures were required until about this time to secure a position as a lighthouse keeper, and some presidents did take an active interest in the nation's lights.[27]

In 1856, as part of the recent reorganization that placed the Lighthouse Bureau in charge of American lights, the Pemaquid Point light received a fourth order Fresnel lens—one of the few of its type in operation today. It required only one lamp—a boon to the keeper. Changes to the lighting system were eventually made at Pemaquid, though its Fresnel lens remains in use.

Part of the information that came out of I.W.P. Lewis's report that helped lead to the reorganization of the bureau involved Pemaquid, as well as a number of lights in the region, and it concerned the possible confusion mariners might experience when traveling in the region. The lighthouses on the Maine coast in general, he said, were often visible for a greater distance during the day than they were at night with their lanterns lit. Buoys and beacons had issues, especially as buoys were often not placed in the most dangerous area along the coastline. (Many were located in river harbors but not in the larger bays and among outlying rocky areas.) Lewis stated quite aggressively that "the mere arrangement of distinguishing lights on the coast of Maine will prove that there is neither knowledge of the wants of navigation, nor any attempt to ascertain those wants."[28]

The view out the window at the base of the tower in summer. *Photo by Trudy Irene Scee.*

Lewis especially found a problem with the lack of variety in the lights in the region that included Pemaquid Point. He wrote, "From Monhegan Island [close to Pemaquid] seven fixed lights are visible in one view," and the sailor could not easily distinguish between them.[29] Pemaquid would have been one of those fixed lights.

According to federal documents, in 1856, the lights at "West Quoddy Head, Prospect Harbor, Eagle Island Point, Negro Island, Dice's Head, Pemaquid Point, Burnt Island, Sequin and Cape Elizabeth" were all "refitted with new and improved reflecting apparatus[es]." This represented a major development on the Maine coastline, and it seems the variations in the lights they sent out were adjusted to reflect Lewis's concerns at the same time, such that a mariner could better locate his or her exact location. The report stated that the new reflecting apparatuses were "designed to serve until suitable lens apparatus can be procured for a final refitment of them."[30] That same year, Pemaquid underwent its final refitment with its Fresnel lens, and changes made thereafter were amazingly few. Accounts of other changes and improvements at Pemaquid Point were included in the 1856 report, with the specific years hand marked on a printed form.

Pemaquid Point Lighthouse

The view over the ocean from the lantern room at the top of the lighthouse tower at Pemaquid. The lantern room is seventy-nine feet above mean sea level, or rather, the focus of its beam is. *Photo by Trudy Irene Scee.*

The light at Pemaquid was part of the first district of the Lighthouse Service after its reorganization. An inspector of lighthouses of the first lighthouse district was stationed at Portland, Maine. Fog signals and buoys were part of the district's jurisdiction, and mariners and others were encouraged to report any problems with the system. The first district continued to stretch from the St. Croix River at the northern border of Maine to the Hampton Harbor in New Hampshire. It included "all aids to navigation on the seacoast of Maine and New Hampshire, and on all tidal waters between the limits names."[31]

The following year, 1857, the government reported that the "Pemaquid Point light-house has been thoroughly repaired and a new keeper's dwelling has been built."[32] This report, like others, was quite brief, but does show that repairs were a constant concern at Pemaquid, as at the other lights. The new dwelling would serve many lightkeepers over the years and is the wooden one that survives today. A photograph from 1857 shows the light station as it was at the time, and it is not so different from now. President James Buchanan had approved the new construction.

The lighthouse service had to ensure that the lighthouse keepers had all they needed to maintain the light stations and to ensure the keepers survival in remote stations, especially in inclement weather. In an example

Pemaquid Point Lighthouse

of supplies sent to the light at Pemaquid in June 1862, the "master of the light house supply vessel, *Pharos*" delivered to the "Pemaquid Fourth Order Light" fifty-one gallons of oil, as there was fifty gallons of oil remaining at the house before the delivery was made. That same June, on the twenty-third, seven rods of hand lamp wicking were delivered as well as, it seems, ten rods of wicking for the light, with twelve rods remaining at the light before the delivery. In addition, nine linen towels, nine pints of "spirits," forty pounds of soap, two lamp chimneys, white wash and various other supplies were delivered. An 1863 receipt shows eighty-six gallons of sperm oil along with three rods of lamp wick being delivered. Keeping the lighthouse supplied was an ongoing process.

In 1867, the keeper's dwelling was repainted, and the following year, government attention focused on the "illuminating apparatus," which was closely examined and needed repairs. Some forty feet of rope and "stove fixer" were supplied to the keeper in one delivery.

Inspections in 1869 showed the light and buildings to be in good repair, without any noticeable work needed. It seems that no major work was undertaken thereafter for over a decade.

Pemaquid Point, circa 1857. The structures are largely unchanged since then, although the keeper's quarters are now white and include a front porch and staircase. *Public Domain.*

By 1881, however, attention was again needed at the Pemaquid Point Light—quite a bit of it. The cellar floor of the keeper's house was cemented, and the roof repaired, primarily on the east side, as was the roof of the "work room." Both roofs were also re-shingled. The outside of the dwelling house was repainted, which required two coats of paint, and the tower itself was repointed.

On January 14, 1889, lighthouse keeper Joseph Lawler wrote to the Office of the Lighthouse Engineer of the First and Second Districts, located in Boston, regarding the boundaries of the Pemaquid Point Lighthouse property. Some confusion had existed as to the true boundaries of the property on which the lighthouse, the workroom and the dwelling were located. Examining surviving letters from the district headquarters sheds some light on the subject, but perhaps not enough.

William H. Stanton responded on January 21, addressing his correspondence to Joseph Lawler at Bristol, Maine: "You wrote to me that when you took charge of the Light Station at Pemaquid Point the fence was on the line B.G.H.C. of the blueprint which is again sent to you herewith, and that there is understood to be a gore of land outside of it belonging to the government." A discussion of where the existing fence was located followed, and a suggestion of exactly where that "gore"—generally a small narrow strip of land, often triangular, and sometimes referring to land that is left out when two surveys do not properly close between two separate properties—might be.

The crux of the problem seems to have been that "the distance given in the Deed for the length of the line B.D., 24 rods [396 feet], will not reach to the bank as it should, according to the Deed." The problem might have been the location of the fence if one were to take measurements from the fence.

Stanton instructed Lawler to "please reply at your earliest convenience, returning the blueprint," and Lawler seemingly did so. Stanton also wrote, "As soon as the weather and roads permit, I will be very glad to get you to go to Pemaquid Point with the surveyor from this office. Please inform me if you can do so. I will pay you a proper amount for your time and expense."

Joseph Lawler apparently wrote back, signifying his willingness to accompany a federal surveyor, a Mr. Adams, as it turned out, to the lighthouse. Lawler was instructed to meet Adams at the stagecoach stop at Bristol on the following Tuesday, January 29.

The issue was unresolved, and since winter is no time to undertake a survey on the rocky coast, on March 8, 1889, the site was surveyed or resurveyed. The boundaries were then marked according to the original deed, dated June

19, 1826. The wording of the 1826 deed seemed to indicate that the property included some bit of land that did not correspond to the actual topography of the location. Some portion of the property used by the government "was never understood to belong to the lighthouse establishment." Following the new survey, the matter was referred to a federal attorney "for adjustment," according to existing letters. The property matter dragged on for some time, and although needed repairs were made at the lighthouse in 1890, the boundary issue was not yet resolved.

In 1892, the matter may have been resolved, as that year, the government constructed a boundary board fence. It also made various repairs, and no further mention of the boundary issue was made in surviving correspondence.

A few years passed and then in 1896, the property saw the addition of a small brick oil house. Situated a little farther down the slope from the light tower and house, the red edifice survives to this day, although it did require some restoration in later years.

Next, in 1897, the U.S. Coast Guard added a brick engine house for a new fog bell, and two steam engines for it were put into use. As described by 1898 lighthouse records, "A fog bell, with duplicated oil-burning steam engines to ring it, was, on September 28, 1897, substituted for the hand bell." A

The oil house. Built in 1896, the house is still standing. *Photo by Trudy Irene Scee.*

weight-driven mechanism drove the new mechanical bell, and there was a small, attached tower containing the weight. The bell house itself would need substantial repairs in the late 1900s, following a severe storm, while the mechanism itself would not remain in operation for long.

Roughly two years after the steam-powered fog bell was installed, "the Shipman fog-signal engines were replaced by a Stevens striking machine, the signal house was adopted to it, and minor repairs were made to the dwelling," according to an 1899 government report. The small tower continued to be used, and the mechanism had to be hand cranked to set it in action. As described later, "The lightkeeper, at the outset of fog or poor visibility, would wind up the Stevens machine, the weights traveling to the top of the tower, and then for the next eight hours, the bell would be struck at regular intervals, the weights slowly descending, much as in a cuckoo clock."[33] A second, smaller bell was installed under the large one for manual use when necessary.

Once the lighthouse began using kerosene for fuel, following the addition of the 1896 oil house, deliveries of kerosene came by way of a tender boat—a supply boat for the lighthouses that brings not just fuel to most of the lights but also all sorts of supplies and sometimes personnel as well. At Pemaquid, the tender would sail as close to the house as possible and throw a fuel line ashore. The fuel could then be pumped in. At Pemaquid, this could be a dicey operation, but no major mishaps occurred. The keepers and the captains knew the weather, the water and the rocks quite well.[34]

According to the Lighthouse Service in 1911, the light at Pemaquid maintained a fifteen-mile visibility across the waters. Listed with other navigation aids, including buoys for the first district, the charts noted that the fog signal consisted of a "bell struck by machinery." The fog signal was one stroke of the bell followed by ten seconds of silence followed by another stroke and ten seconds of silence and so forth. The fourth order fixed lens in its white tower and was specified as being, "on SE'ly point of rock, W'ly side of entrance to Muscongus Bay." The light station was largely unchanged since the 1830s—only the emphasis had shifted such that it was primarily considered a light guarding the Muscongus Bay, with Johns Bay left out of the description. The nearby New Harbor Sunken Ledges Buoy was listed next on the list of navigation aids. Interestingly, the current inspector for the district was then headquartered at the YMCA building in Portland, Maine.[35]

The lighthouse board began testing the use of electricity at lighthouses in about 1900. The process took decades, however, and all lights were not electrified until the 1940s, although most were converted by the 1930s—

Left: The bell tower in the late 1990s, not long after it was repaired following a hurricane. *Photo by Trudy Irene Scee.*

Right: The replacement smaller fog bell at Pemaquid Point in 2018. It hangs at almost the edge of the cliff. *Photo by Trudy Irene Scee.*

some through the use of generators. Once electricity arrived, the keeper no longer had to haul kerosene or other fuels up the spiral staircase; he had only to change the electric bulbs as they wore out. Although cleaning and polishing the apparatus and the glass of the tower remained duties of the keeper, there was no soot with electric bulbs and no smoke—just a switch to turn on and off. At Pemaquid the keeper continued to carry gas or kerosene up the spiral staircase right up until the light was automated on October 1, 1934. In the process, the fuel supply switched to acetylene gas, which the Lighthouse Service started to use in selected lights in 1902 and 1903 but which did not see widespread use for several years.[36]

Established in the 1820s and automated in the mid-1930s, the Pemaquid Point lighthouse saw its share of deaths and rescues. Lightkeepers, from the beginning to the end of their time at Pemaquid and throughout the history of the manning of the light, found their work challenging, rewarding and dangerous. Some chose to stay at the station as long as they could while

Postcard of visitors enjoying the rocks at Pemaquid, circa 1912. These people were actually in a dangerous position on the ledge. *Courtesy of the Fisherman's Museum.*

others chose to move on to other lights. Some came to the station with a family while others created families there. Yet others lived alone, tending the light and performing the many duties of the station alone or with other help as they could find it.

Later years would see various changes at the lighthouse, but in the meantime, the crashing waves continued to cause deaths and injuries, as people were knocked down or swept to sea on those same beautiful rocks that make the location so unique and enticing. For Pemaquid never lost its appeal—not in any season nor in any year.

BRASSWORK
OR
THE LIGHTHOUSE KEEPER'S LAMENT

By Fred Morong
Born Lubec Maine, 1883, district machinist starting 1922

Oh what is the bane of a lightkeeper's life
That causes him worry, struggle and strife,
That makes him use cuss words, and beat at his wife?
It's Brasswork.

What makes him look ghastly, consumptive and thin,
What robs him of breath, of vigor and vim,
And causes despair and drives him to sin?
It's Brasswork.

The devil himself could never invent,
A material causing more world wide lament,
And in Uncle Sam's service about ninety per cent,
Is Brasswork.

The lamp in the tower, reflector and shade,
The tools and accessories pass in parade.
As a matter of fact the whole outfit is made
Of Brasswork.

The oil containers I polish until
My poor back is broken, aching; and still
Each gallon and quart, each pint and gill
Is Brasswork.

I lay down to slumber all weary and sore,
I walk in my sleep, I awake with a snore
And I'm shining the knob on my bedroom door,
That's Brasswork.

From pillar to post, rags and polish I tote.
I'm never without them, for you will please note
That even the buttons I wear on my coat
Are Brasswork.

The machinery, clockwork, and fog-signal bell,
The coal hods, the dustpans, the pump in the well
Now I'll leave it you mates, if this isn't—well
Brasswork.

I dig, scrub and polish, and work with a might,
And just when I get it all shining bright,
In comes the fog like a thief in the night:
Good-by Brasswork.

I start the next day and when noontime draws near,
A boatload of Summer visitors appear,
For no other purpose, than to smooch and besmear
My Brasswork.

So it goes all the Summer, and along in the Fall,
Comes the district machinist to overhaul
And rub dirty and greasy paws all over
My Brasswork.

And again in the Spring, if perchance it may be,
An efficiency star is awarded to me
I open the package and what do I see?
More Brasswork.

Oh, why should the spirit of mortal be proud,
In the short span of life that he is allowed
If all the lining in every dark cloud
Is Brasswork?

And when I have polished until I am cold
And I'm taken aloft to the Heavenly fold
Will my harp and my crown be made of pure gold?
No, Brasswork.

3

THE LIGHTKEEPERS OF PEMAQUID

Lightkeepers were sometimes romanticized, sometimes deemed people who lived monotonous and lonely lives; the truth was most likely different for each person who undertook the unmistakably difficult lightkeeper's job in the early 1800s. Even later, when changes in the lighting apparatus and in transportation to and from the lights and other advances occurred, the work remained difficult and often solitary. That is not to say that it was unrewarding, and the beauty of places like Pemaquid Point may have added special benefits, even as they presented their own challenges.

The secretary of the treasury theoretically chose every lightkeeper during the era when Pemaquid was built, but in general, keepers would be selected at the local level. Presidents also might have a say in the matter, especially up to the 1840s, but they generally left the details to others. But even at Pemaquid, there were exceptions, and the president did sometimes get involved.

There were female keepers in the United States, and a few women in Maine served as assistant keepers but not at Pemaquid. There were women who lived there, but they did not serve as head or salaried lighthouse keepers. There would be only fourteen long-term keepers, all told, at Pemaquid Point, and they would all be men.

Lightkeepers at Pemaquid, as elsewhere, had to light the lamps—there might be many wicks or candles and even lamps involved—at dusk and extinguish them again at dawn. They had to sound the horns or ring the bell in fog, depending on the decade. They had to clean those bells and horns and lamps and keep lenses and reflecting apparatus clean and in good

Pemaquid Point Lighthouse

Left: The rocks in the late 1990s, looking up. The rock formation has changed little in the last few hundred years. *Photo by Trudy Irene Scee.*

Below: The tower and lighthouse from the opposite side in the 1800s. *Public domain and courtesy of the Fisherman's Museum.*

order. They had to polish all the brass in the light room. They had to keep the wicks refreshed, trimming and replacing them as needed. They had to carry sperm oil, possibly lard for a few years and, later, kerosene and then gas up the many steps to the tower. The steps at Pemaquid are steep, ending in a short iron ladder and a sharp twist to reach the lamp or lantern room, which has little space to negotiate one's self, never mind gallons of oil, lard, kerosene or gas. And the keepers had to be certain that every one of those steps remained safe and in good repair.[37]

Lightkeepers also had to keep the glass surrounding the light room clear, both inside and out, and that could be hazardous work. Ice and snow on the glass could prove fatal to those trusting the light to guide them. The iron gallery at Pemaquid Point provided a platform for cleaning the glass, but it could be a cold, wet, windy, slippery and dangerous platform in inclement weather. Soot was a problem in all seasons during many of the decades, so it needed to be cleaned regularly by the lightkeeper all year. Any broken glass needed to be replaced immediately.

Although not perched directly on the cliff, the lighthouse is close enough, and the oil house is even closer, although at a less steep location, so slipping could prove extremely dangerous. If one slid, one could indeed go over the edge or tumble many feet to land on the unyielding granite and craggy stones below. And the bell house is even closer; indeed, it is on the very edge of the cliff and the ledge that runs out from it, and the current bell essentially hangs over the cliff.

Although larger construction projects might be handled by one of the lighthouse services or districts depending on the year, the lightkeeper was expected to keep the entire light station clean and in proper condition. The first keeper at Pemaquid, Isaac Dunham, oversaw the construction of the 1835 tower and lived with the results and problems of the original 1827 tower. He approved the second construction job when it was finished and reported on the work to the lighthouse service. Dunham improved the lighting apparatus's functioning in cold weather and would serve as the keeper from November 3, 1827, until Nathaniel Gamage Jr. replaced him on June 13, 1837, not long after the new tower saw completion.

In 1914, J. Henry Cartland would write that keeper Dunham's grandson, Martin V.B. Dunham, owned a small island at the entrance to New Harbor near the northeastern edge of Pemaquid Point and had a small cottage there, while Charles E. Marr and his family had the keep of Pemaquid Point Lighthouse, followed by Charles A. Dolliver and Herman E. Brewer. (Brewer seems to have been at the light for less than a year and was perhaps

Keepers, sea captains and visitors liked to pose by the lighthouse once photography became a viable option in the later 1800s. *Photo from Pemaquid Point Lighthouse Collections.*

a temporary keeper or an assistant during the transition from Dolliver to Marr.) Cartland also found it worth mentioning that the fog bell was a "large" one.[38] Indeed, such bells could weigh over a ton.

The tower at Pemaquid, as true for other masonry ones in Maine and other colder climates, had to be kept free of cracks for general maintenance reasons and to keep the tower and the fuel as warm as possible. In cold weather, the keeper had to make certain that the fuel, especially oil and lard, did not congeal or thicken; it had to be the proper temperature to burn. Everything had to be done to keep the light as bright as possible, and this is where Dunham's improvement came to be important. The light, above all, was critical. It was the light that could save lives, although at Pemaquid, the bright white tower itself provided a visual aid in clear daylight hours. The rocks at Pemaquid protrude into the ocean, the waves are often rough and a miscalculation could easily bring disaster, as time demonstrated, even with diligent care by the keeper. Less than diligent care would likely have cost more people their lives.

Of course, the keeper had to take care of his own life to make sure that he and his family or partner, if he had one, had enough food and fuel and other necessities to weather the winters and storms. He had to plan ahead for his own needs, as well as for the light station's. In the early decades, when there was less oversight and organization with the governing bodies, this was especially critical. The lightkeeper also had to keep meticulous records. This was true throughout the history of the light at Pemaquid Point.

Most of the Pemaquid keepers did have wives and families to help with the work and to keep loneliness at bay. A child or wife of the keeper might learn all the duties involved in keeping the light, perhaps with more understanding than a new person coming in. But as the years passed, securing the position of lighthouse keeper proved more difficult, especially after the Lighthouse Board was established in the 1850s and after the Coast Guard assumed control of American lights in 1939, when one might be a visiting lightkeeper and share duties at more than one light. Even earlier, during the first few decades of the lights in the Pemaquid region, the positions were sometimes politically appointed. And one could be replaced on a moment's notice by an acquaintance or stranger with a note in his hands saying that the job was now his or hers.

After the reorganization of the Lighthouse Bureau, a person had to be between the ages of eighteen and fifty to serve as a lighthouse keeper. They had to be able to read, write and keep books, which, actually, they had needed to be able to do all along to perform their duties. The bureau also started a lending library, with each light station receiving a number of books for a few months and then sending them off in exchange for a new packet of books. The lighthouse provisioner, a regular position after the 1850s changes were implemented, would bring them. More changes called for in 1852 might take some time to be enacted in outposts, including Pemaquid Point.

Pemaquid had at least fourteen recognized keepers before it was fully automated. It also had a visiting keeper for some time after the reorganization, as well as various caretakers.

Keepers worked long and varied hours for their pay at Pemaquid, according to some specific original records. In the mid-1800s, the district

Keeping the light provisioned was a serious matter at Pemaquid and the other Maine lighthouses. In some cases, lightkeepers exchanged their own produce and products for other goods, and in some cases, they depended on local fishermen and small stores to secure what supplies the tender ships did not bring. *Photo from Pemaquid Point Lighthouse Collections.*

headquarters took charge of salaries, and the superintendent of lights submitted vouchers to secure the keeper's pay. In 1861, for example, Jedediah Jewett submitted one of his quarterly vouchers—$39.97 for the Pemaquid Point keeper's pay. Another one for $39.99 also survives. There may have been small variations due to amounts subtracted for any personal supplies. Although these were submitted on quarterly report forms, they were actually for one month of pay.[39]

Federal sources indicate that the first keeper, Isaac Dunham, who started in 1827, was paid $350 per year, and Robert Curtis, who started at the light in 1849, also earned $350 per year. Joseph Lawler started his duties at the light in March 1861, and the surviving receipts were for his pay.[40] Pemaquid was not the mostly highly paid position in Maine, however, and that may have played a role in how long some keepers stayed at the station.

As noted, lighthouse keepers needed to keep good records, especially as the years went by. These included lists of supplies needed and received, the numbers and types of vessels passing by and accounts of shipwrecks and other events. Together, these records also show how life was for specific

Pemaquid Point Lighthouse

The two towers of Pemaquid—the light tower at the top of the cliff and the bell tower a little west of and below it. *Photo by Trudy Irene Scee.*

keepers and specific lights. Surviving records from Pemaquid Point are interesting and informative. Lightkeepers' names have been added, though they did not always appear.

In 1863, for example, a list of supplies received during one shipment highlights the materials needed for day-to-day maintenance. Jonathan Howland served as the master of the supply ship at the time and delivered most of the provisions needed. In mid-July 1863, he brought a long list of items to the light. First on the list, and a very telling item in its exact type and quantity, was "eighty-six gals. of sperm oil." Sperm oil was used to keep the light going, as was the next item, "ten rds. 4th order wix." In addition, "three rods lamp wicking," eight linen towels, "two pts. spirit wine," soap, lamp black, "polishing powder," a record book for ship sightings, "one sweeping brush," writing paper, "one box wafers," steel pens, "one lead pencil," twenty-four slate pencils, "twelve large envelopes," "four official envelopes," "one slate" and "one writing box" were delivered, as were a few other items.[41] There was nothing unexpected in the list of provisions delivered that June, and all of those listed could be seen as directly used in tending the light, except perhaps the wafers, depending on what type they were.

The keepers of the light at Pemaquid, as elsewhere, also needed personal supplies for themselves and any family they might have. In the early years, this could prove a challenge, and when purchases involved governmental charges, meticulous records of purchases for foodstuffs were maintained. The keeper might also have a monthly or other allowance for things like coal for house stoves.

Records from 1869—with the light recorded as being in the district of Portland and Falmouth, a subdivision—show some of the foodstuffs and other goods used personally by the keeper and his family. For example, an account of hens and eggs under the heading "Credit by Eggs" was kept in a journal issued by the district's lighthouse inspector. The journal includes the number of eggs sold and the price for each sale. In another example, bushels of corn and other foodstuffs were recorded.[42] It may be that the keeper was not buying some of these foodstuffs but selling them, especially with the credit by eggs account, as during some years, keepers did keep domestic animals.

In April 1874, the keeper noted purchases, or sales, of three pounds six ounces of butter, followed by four pounds eight ounces, three pounds twelve ounces and then another three pounds. The keeper seems to have been using (or selling) three to four pounds of butter a week or stocking up on it. Butter

The ledges on the western side of the peninsula near Pemaquid Point. This is near where the author once stayed with her brother. *Photo by Trudy Irene Scee.*

records survive from November 1880 to November 1881 and show no great surprises or variations from the 1874 records.[43]

Keepers also recorded the number of ships passing by "in the vicinity" of the lighthouse on forms provided by the government from the mid-1800s on. The name of each lighthouse and the date were filled in by hand, as were the various types of vessels spotted.

A surviving form for Pemaquid Point, for example, shows that during the quarter ending June 30, 1866, in April alone, nine ships, one bark, twenty-four brigs, 225 schooners, one sloop and fourteen steamers were sighted by the lightkeeper and others, for a total of 340 vessels. The keeper sent the report to Commodore John Pope, the lighthouse inspector of the

Pemaquid Point Lighthouse

The bell tower as it was before automation with one of the last keepers, shown wearing his uniform and holding a spyglass. Just visible below the large bell is the smaller one, mounted for manual use when necessary. *Public Domain.*

first district. Records seem to indicate that this was the busiest month of the season.[44]

As noted, Isaac Dunham served as Pemaquid Point's first lightkeeper, starting his duties the day that the original tower and lamps went into duty, November 29, 1827. Dunham was forty years old at the time and had been working as a farmer in Maine since the War of 1812. He was born in Plymouth, Massachusetts, and had gone to sea before he moved to Maine. His father, Captain Cornelius Dunham, had commanded numerous ships, so Dunham's career choices were natural, given his background. According to federal records, he earned $350 a year for his services.

Dunham married Abigail Cary and had five children with her before they moved to Pemaquid Point. A son, Benjamin, was born in February 1831, at the lighthouse station. Decades later, in 1868, another baby, Susie, was born at the house to Sophronia and Joseph Lawler while the Lawlers tended the station.

Isaac Dunham's father came to stay at Pemaquid Point. He died at Pemaquid in July 1835 and was buried nearby. His stone remains not too far from the lighthouse, with his years of life marked as 1746 through 1832 and the inscription "Capt. Cornelius Dunham, who was father of Isaac Dunham, the first keeper of Pemaquid Light." His son's burial spot, however, is unknown. When Dunham left Pemaquid in 1849, he transferred to the Minot's Ledge Light off the coast of Cohasset, Massachusetts, south of Boston. This was a light tower built on iron stilts. His son went with him as an assistant keeper. Isaac Dunham earned $600 a year as head keeper at the new light.[45]

It was Isaac Dunham who, as the first lightkeeper at Minot's Ledge, wrote to Washington, D.C., requesting that the light be strengthened. He had lost his young cat during a storm, when the tower tipped so drastically the kitten jumped or fell into the ocean after first landing on the rocks below. In another storm, he wrote in his journal that the sea and gusts moving the tower about made him feel like a "Drunken Man—I hope God will in mercy still the raging sea—or we must perish." He also wrote to the service about the safety of the light.[46]

Dunham resigned on October 7, 1850, when his requests went unanswered. The next keeper initially laughed at his concerns and then experienced a few of his own. The light at Minot's Ledge crashed into the sea during a storm on April 16, 1851, and it took the assistant keepers on duty with it into the ocean. Knowing it was about to happen, they had pounded on the bell for as long as they could and put a message into a sealed bottle. The sound of the bell was heard, but no help could arrive. Fortunately for Dunham, his son, also Isaac Dunham, had left when he did, along with his other assistant keeper.[47]

Dunham kept domestic animals, including chickens, at the light station on Pemaquid, as did a number of the other keepers, as indicated by surviving records. It is likely that sheep were also kept at or very near the station, according to one source, and the flock would later, in the early twentieth century, be moved to a nearby island.[48]

It became the custom of the lightkeepers of Pemaquid to keep not just a few animals and a small vegetable plot, as was common, but to actually maintain a small farm associated with their position. According to Edward Rowe Snow in *The Lighthouses of New England*, first published in 1945, Dunham eventually constructed a few buildings and barns, which he deemed worth some $1,100 when he was transferred in 1837. He then asked the incoming keeper, Nathaniel Gamage, to pay him for the improvements he had made. Gamage paid as requested. The next keeper, however, was not so agreeable about the arrangement.[49]

Gamage would serve for four years and then be replaced by Jeremiah S. Mears (also spelled as Means in some sources), purportedly for solely political reasons. Newly elected president Benjamin Harrison replaced Gamage with Mears in 1841. Presidents did have the final say, as noted, in lighthouse appointments. Mears, however, did not want to pay the assessed value of the farming improvements at the light. He agreed to pay Gamage rent for the use of the property, but Gamage was not satisfied with this offer. He appealed to President John Tyler, who had replaced Harrison as president upon Harrison's death. Tyler asked the secretary of the treasury, John Spencer, to look into the matter. Spencer was able to reach an agreement between the two men in which Mears would pay Gamage outright if a fair appraisal was made, but Gamage continued to complain that Mears had not even made payments as originally agreed on. In July 1843, Gamage said that the only way to satisfactorily resolve the matter was to reinstate him as the Pemaquid lightkeeper, but this did not happen.[50]

Mears stayed at Pemaquid for a while and then moved on. Robert Curtis would serve as the keeper starting in July 1849, at a yearly salary of $350, and Samuel C. Tibbets started as keeper in April 1853, also at $350. In February 1858, John Fossett took on the appointment. Three years later, in late March 1861, Joseph Lawler became the lightkeeper at Pemaquid and would stay there for several years. Surviving records show him receiving $39.79 for one month of service during 1861, although some lighthouse records indicate that a keeper might be paid quarterly.[51]

View from the western side of the point and the lighthouse as a late season storm started to set in. *Photo by Trudy Irene Scee.*

In July 1869, Marcus A. Hanna became the keeper at Pemaquid. Born in November 1842 in Bristol, Hanna was a local boy by birth but actually grew up at the Franklin Island Lighthouse, where his parents, Eliza and James Hanna, were the keepers. He went to sea as a youth, was in the navy at the outbreak of the Civil War and served in some voluntary infantry groups. Hanna returned to Bristol and married Louise, or Louisiana, Davis shortly after the war ended. The two piloted a small boat and supplied fish to a market until Marcus Hannah became the keeper at Pemaquid. During the next few winters, when they were not directly involved in tending the light, the two taught at the local school. Marcus Hanna did not stay at the Pemaquid lighthouse for long, though. He requested a more desirable post, and in 1873, President Ulysses Grant, his former general, transferred him to the Two Lights station on Cape Elizabeth.[52]

At Hanna's transfer, the outgoing keeper of Two Lights wrote in the station's log, "Mr. Hanna from Pemaquid Light Station will take my place but not with my consent. I am no longer a Republican." He left the entry there, knowing, of course, that Hanna would see it.[53] He apparently resented what he saw as his own loss of position at Cape Elizabeth for what he deemed political reasons and seemingly intended to leave the political party of the president.

On January 28, 1885, while at Two Lights, Hanna braved a blizzard to rescue two men from the schooner *Australia*. Their ship, which had sailed out of Boothbay Harbor just southwest of Pemaquid and was loaded with ice and mackerel to take to Boston, had wrecked on the rocks below the station light. (As at Pemaquid, the towers at Two Light were constructed on a cliff—or hill—above the ocean.) Louise Hanna had spotted the two survivors when she climbed one of the towers the next morning to extinguish the light.[54]

Marcus Hanna was able—after breaking into an iced-over outbuilding in the four-degree (or less) temperature to get line and metal for a hook and then heaving himself over the rocks in deep snow and ice—to get a line out to the ship. The first stranded man tied the line around himself and then jumped into the water. Hanna pulled him to shore and then threw the line to the second man. Additional workers had come by that time, and they helped pull the second man in. The rescuers brought the men to the fog signal house, cut their frozen clothes off and worked to warm and revive them.[55]

Although the rescue did not occur at Pemaquid, the incident demonstrates the many, often unexpected, situations a lighthouse keeper might encounter. Shipwrecks were not the only times a keeper might have to respond to an emergency, although Pemaquid would see its share of those, and the waves

Pemaquid Point Lighthouse

Early winter at Pemaquid Point. Wreaths are placed along the fence for the Christmas and holiday season. One is visible in the foreground, as is the bell donated by the Coast Guard. *Photo by Trudy Irene Scee.*

at Pemaquid have swept more than one person into the ocean. Hanna received the Gold Lifesaving Metal that April for rescuing the men. He later received a Medal of Honor for his bravery while serving in the Civil War. He is the only person to have received both prestigious awards—one the highest military award and the other the highest civilian award for bravery in the United States.[56] Meanwhile, back at Pemaquid, William Sartell had come to serve as the new keeper at Pemaquid.

The reasons Hanna left Pemaquid are not all known, but economic and cultural factors are likely. Cape Elizabeth is closer to a larger community, as it is near Portland, and the married couple may have felt isolated at Pemaquid, although the area did have small towns even then. Working at Two Lights also paid more, as it had from the beginning. While in the early years, keepers at Pemaquid were making $350 per year, those at Two Lights made $450, which increased to $500, while the keepers at Pemaquid were still receiving $350. This was a large difference in pay scale. Inflation was not a critical issue during these years, and the divergent rates were clearly significant. However, there were two lights at Two Lights, so the workload was significantly larger.[57] But the keeper at Two Lights, or Cape Elizabeth Station, as records were often filed, had help.

Louise Davis Hanna helped with the work at Cape Elizabeth, and she likely did at Pemaquid as well. Indeed, although there have been no recognized female primary lightkeepers in Maine, Louise Hanna did, at some point, enter into a separate agreement with the Lighthouse Service. (She was not the only woman in Maine to do so.) The service has records of her severing her agreement and resigning from her post at Cape Elizabeth. In the box for names, the service had "Hanna, Mrs. Loui[s]e" and the category as "Third Assistant of Cape Elizabeth Light Station," classified as "tenders her resignation."[58]

Louise Davis was one of the many women in the United States who would serve at one or more lights in various capacities but would never be appointed head lightkeeper. Of course, Louise Davis may not have wanted the appointment, and it is quite likely that she resigned her duties at Cape Elizabeth as her husband, Marcus Hanna, resigned his in late 1885—the year of the rescue—after first spending another storm manually ringing the fog bell. Marcus died in 1921, at age seventy-nine, and Louise died in 1936. They were buried in Portland. In 1997, the U.S. Coast Guard named a tender for Marcus Hanna.[59]

Judging from the federal records, the post at Pemaquid was a competitive one. Several Lighthouse Service records indicate that there were a number

Pemaquid Point Lighthouse

A view of the lighthouse during another early winter. *Photo by Trudy Irene Scee.*

Even one hundred years ago, keepers had to worry about visitors getting too close to the water. Postcard circa 1912. *Courtesy of the Fisherman's Museum.*

of applicants for the job right from the beginning. Records show there were "bundled recommendations" for Isaac Dunham in March 1827. A number of men had entries in the records during the spring of 1827—both before and after Dunham had his in and before the light was built. Later, the service would note that personnel had "bundled recommendations and applications of various candidates. Dated '1828' and filed at the beginning of the year," pertaining to applications for the keeper's job. Stephen Pleasonton, the U.S. Treasury auditor, whose reign over the lighthouse service would later be called into question, had actually recommended one of Dunham's competitor's, Esais Preble, for the position.[60]

Specifically, Pleasonton wrote to President Adams on August 20, 1827:

> *Sir;*
> *The Superintendent having reported that the Lighthouse on Pemaquid Point, in Maine, would be completed in about three weeks from the 13th instant, I have the honor to enclose the recommendations in favor of the following persons to be Keeper thereof, viz: Esaias Preble, John Lennan, Isaac Dunham, Josiah Dunham, Norton P. Parsons, David Vose, Jacob Sherburn, Paul McCobb, Henry R. Myers, William Garret, Henry Works, Robert Henderson, Samuel Moody, John Upham, Joshua Palmer, Zaccheus Trafton, Samuel Davis, Samuel Holmes, John Martin, Herman Smith, David Hooper, Patrick Mahoney and John S. Blake. The appointment of Esaias Preble is respectfully submitted, and that his salary be fixed at three hundred and fifty years per annum.*
> *I am, S. Pleasonton*
> *Fifth Auditor and Act. Com. Of the Rev.*[61]

Pleasonton had included Isaac Dunham as one of the twenty-three men to be considered, but Preble was clearly his first choice. The recommended salary would be the one Isaac Dunham would receive, though. And it seems that one of Dunham's relatives had also applied for the job. In following years, the post would remain competitive.

William S. Sartell earned $560 a year when he took over the keeper's job at Pemaquid Point from Marcus Hanna in 1873, while Marcus earned $720 a year at Cape Elizabeth, and Louise (again spelled Louis in government records) earned $400. She seems to have assumed the duties of an assistant keeper upon their move or soon thereafter. This would have been a substantial increase in their family income. Furthermore, during the same period, a James T. Hanna made $420 a year, while Harry S. Libby made $500 a year at Cape Elizabeth.[62]

Pemaquid Point Lighthouse

The eastern side of the tower, showing the slope down to the ocean. *Photo by Trudy Irene Scee.*

View from the lantern room at the top of the tower to the eastern side of the premises. *Photo by Trudy Irene Scee.*

The point at sunset. *Photo by Trudy Irene Scee.*

By the time Charles Dolliver—born in Maine like Hanna—worked as the Pemaquid keeper in the early 1880s, the starting salary was $500 per year, while Marcus Hanna then earned $720 and "Mrs. Louie A. Hanna" earned $420 at Cape Elizabeth. The other personnel at the lighthouse had changed by the time the pertinent report came out. The head keeper at nearby Sequin Island, much closer to Pemaquid, earned $700 a year and had assistants, while at the neighboring Marshall Point Light, the keeper made $500. Dolliver's salary soon increased to $560, according to federal records. Salary raises did come to those who came and stayed at the Pemaquid Light, but it did not equal that of the larger stations.[63]

It was during Dolliver's time as the keeper of the Pemaquid Light that uniforms became mandatory. Keepers Dunham, Gamage, Means, Curtis, Fossett, Lawler, Hanna and Sartell had been able to wear pretty much whatever they wished during their tenures, although the service would have wanted them to present a neat appearance. In 1883, however, the Lighthouse Board decided that that freedom of dress needed to change.

The board declared that it wanted lighthouse personnel to begin wearing uniforms, as "it is believed that uniforming the personnel of the service… will aid in maintaining its discipline, increase its efficiency, raise its tone, and add to the *esprit de corps*." Therefore, starting in May 1884, male keepers had to wear uniforms. A female keeper uniform was never created.[64]

Male keepers and other personnel were now required to wear a uniform consisting of "coat, vest, and trousers and a cap or helmet." The coat was to be double breasted, with pockets and five buttons on each side—the top two being hidden by the collar. The vest was to be navy blue and have pockets for a watch and other goods, five buttons and a collar that would show about five inches of the shirt underneath. Trousers would also be navy blue, as would the cap. The guidelines were quite specific, and the buttons of various sizes had to be according to regulation. The principle keeper of a light would have a *K* worn on a gold loop on his coat. Uniform materials could vary according to the season. The buttons, made of "triple gilt on brass," had lighthouses on them and were the source of some of the polishing lament on the poem written about the woes of brass in the lightkeeper's life. Keepers were to wear their uniforms whenever they were on duty.[65]

Maine and Pemaquid might seem far away from the bustle of the national headquarters to some people, but keepers were subject to inspection and had to be ready for it at any time. Moreover, there was a system by which people progressed in the service, especially after the 1850s, and it applied to those who wanted to work at Pemaquid, as well as those who might want to leave service. As later explained by the erudite wife of one of the Maine keepers, "There were definite steps to advancement in the Lighthouse Service. First or second assistant keepers were assigned to remote and isolated stations. After proving they could successfully survive this probation period, they could select the station they would accept a transfer to."[66]

The writer of this statement, Connie Scovill Small, said that she and her husband, Elson, would spread charts on the floor to look over the possibilities. They would, she recounted, go to two of the places they picked.[67]

In 1899, Charles Dolliver would leave Pemaquid Point to become the head keeper at Maine's Goose Rock Light, a "spark plug light" completely surrounded by water. However, he seems to have moved on from there fairly quickly. At the end or overlapping the end of Dolliver's time at Pemaquid, there seem to have been two men who briefly served as assistants to the keeper or as temporary keepers: Rufus McKinney Jr. in 1898 and Herbert E. Brewer in parts of 1898 and 1899.

Clarence E. Marr would come to Pemaquid Point as its head keeper in 1899 and stay until 1922, serving for twenty-three years. Marr's was an eventful tenure at the light, with the worst tragedy to date striking the point in 1903. Marr came to the light with experience, including in aiding shipwrecked schooners.[68]

Marr was born in 1852, at what one might call the height of nineteenth-century lighthouse building and had a father and a brother who were lighthouse keepers at Hendricks Head Light near Southport, Maine, south of Boothbay Harbor. Marr's father, Captain Jaruel Marr, had started as keeper there in 1866 with his wife, Catherine, when Clarence was fourteen years old. He was purportedly given the post as a reward for his bravery in the Civil War. Clarence's brother, Wolcott Marr, also became a lighthouse keeper, starting in 1890, as an assistant keeper at Two Lights at Cape Elizabeth at age nineteen. In 1895, when his father retired, he succeeded him at Hendrick's Head.[69]

Clarence Marr had been an assistant keeper the Cuckolds Fog and Light Station—a colorful name for a station located on an island south of Boothbay fairly close to Pemaquid Point—before he came to work at Pemaquid as its keeper. Marr had served as an assistant keeper at Pemaquid from 1896 until 1898 and as head keeper at Cuckholds in 1898 and 1899.[70]

On January 4, 1896, while he was at Cuckholds Lighthouse, the schooner *Aurora*, sailing out of Nova Scotia, came to a "mishap" near the light, and Clarence Marr and his fellow keeper, E.H. Pierce, rescued the captain and crew at some risk to their own lives. The Canadian government recognized their bravery and wished to award the men with silver watches. U.S. naval secretary commander George F.F. Wilde reported that the department would be passing the recommendation to Washington so the men might receive the watches from the Canadian government, but it took some time for the watches to reach them—about four years. By that time, Marr and his wife, Clara E., had moved to Pemaquid and were on the eve of another fateful event. Marr served at Pemaquid with an initial salary of $500. A Maine congressman also recommend that Pierce and Marr be given the Lighthouse Board's Life Saving Gold or Silver Medal, but it seems that did not happen.[71]

After serving for four years at Avery Rock in Machias Bay, which had opened in 1875 at the northeast end of Maine, as well as a stint as head keeper at Two Bush Island Light from 1919 until 1925 and as an assistant from 1916 until 1919 in the Penobscot Bay, in mid-1926, Elson Small was asked to take charge of the three-man station on Sequin Island. On the way there, where the Smalls would live for another four years, Connie Small recounted that at Pemaquid and at some of the other lights, the keeper and his family, especially the children, would go out and wave at the boat. The service required that keepers respond to the "tender's salute." And as she noted, if a keeper was away "on a family light, a member of the family was expected to take over"—both responding to salutes and other duties—and "no extra money was paid for this service."[72] It is not surprising that Mrs. Hanna, who had been stationed at Pemaquid with her husband before moving to Cape Elizabeth, had signed on for pay for her duties. Clara E. Marr and the other women who moved to the Pemaquid Light no doubt performed invaluable services as well.

At Pemaquid, as elsewhere, a wife might be expected to tend the light when her husband was unable do so for whatever reason. She was also expected to help in other ways at the station. The federal government might not call for that service directly, but it was anticipated—it was part of most keeper families' way of life.

A *Lewiston Journal* article on file at the Maine State Library dated February 2, 1924, discusses some of the events at Pemaquid and includes a photograph of a couple identified as "Mr. and Mrs. Robinson, Keepers of Pemaquid Light." Henry Robinson had come to Pemaquid from the Monhegan Light, although his name did not appear on initial lists of lighthouse keepers at Pemaquid. The rather blurred photograph shows a couple standing by the large fog bell then in use at Pemaquid (more like the one now in the yard than the smaller one currently mounted on the building), the man sporting a moustache and cap and wearing what appear to be overalls but may have been his uniform and the woman, Isabella, standing stoically at his side wearing a long dark coat or fitted cape and a light-colored dress. She seems to have bangs with the rest of her hair pulled up.[73]

The article stated that the Robinsons were fine hosts and that the visitor received "unbounded cheer" at their home. Indeed, the author of the piece, G.W. Singer, although he had arrived by land, stated, "Were we to be shipwrecked anywhere we'd prefer to be flung ashore at Pemaquid Light. The Robinsons would save one from the sea if anyone could, and the kind attentions afterward would compensate for the danger encountered. The coffee, the eggs and bacon, minced pie and jellies with which they greet the stranger would almost be worth a shipwreck."[74]

Singer exaggerated a bit, as no one would trade a shipwreck for good coffee—even when served with pie—but his statements do support the often-expressed claim by keepers in the later decades that entertaining visitors was part of their job. In the summer season after the mid- to late 1800s in particular, visitors could be numerous at locations like Pemaquid, which would see a number of hotels nearby by the 1910s.

Pemaquid Point Lighthouse

Herbert Robinson had served Libby Island as its first assistant keeper when Clarence Marr was serving for $500 a year at Pemaquid. Robinson's service dates at Libby Island were 1902 until 1905, and he earned $480 during at least one, if not all, of those years. Later records show him serving at the Monhegan Light as the head keeper from 1919 until 1922. At that point, he was transferred to Pemaquid Point, when Clarence Marr retired from service. Born in 1852, Marr had had a long career at Maine lights. Robinson, too, would have a long service career, and his daughter would be married on the porch at Pemaquid Point.[75]

Isabella Robinson generated some publicity on her own behalf. She was "a naval veteran of the Great War." She had served officially during World War I. Some women associated with lighthouses had enlisted in the U.S. Navy during the war, including one of the women then serving at Cape Elizabeth, and were stationed at their light. Isabella Robinson had, no matter her official position, been at the Moose Peake Naval Station (one of several Maine lights, including Pemaquid, declared at U.S. Naval lookout station during the war), where she injured her arm. Her hand had been crippled, and more serious consequences might yet occur, including, coverage seemed to imply, an amputation. Isabella Robinson kept an "official recognition of her service framed and hanging on the wall of her house,"[76] according to the *Lewiston Journal*. Certainly, this was something the lighthouse service inspectors would have considered "up to snuff."

Before then, Isabella Robinson had served with her husband at Moose Peak and Pemaquid Point, and their daughter, Inez Robinson Ingalls, also married a lightkeeper. Disaster struck when Inez's husband, Eugene Ingalls, the keeper at Petit Manan Lighthouse since 1914, left to meet her in a powerboat at Moose Peak, where she was visiting her parents on December 29, 1916, and was lost at sea. His boat was eventually found but not his body.[77] Potential tragedy was not confined to the home for the lightkeeper—travels to see family or to secure goods could also be dangerous.

The condition of the keeper's house continued to be part of lighthouse inspections over the years. In the 1920s and for some time after, the lighthouse service would grant a star to each station that passed its inspection. The lights that passed inspections for three consecutive years would be awarded a commissioner's star. A light that achieved that status and continued to improve might be awarded a district pendant.[78]

Lightkeepers and any family they might have were expected to keep their homes, towers and the rest of the stations in meticulous condition. Inspections of the light tower generally included the keeper's dwelling. A tender for the lights—a variety of supply boats were used before 1939 and known as tenders—might bring not only food, fuel and other supplies but also, without warning, lighthouse personnel. The arrival of such a boat could prove both exciting and worrisome. At Pemaquid, a land-based light, most goods and personnel could be brought overland, which meant that lighthouse personnel could appear at almost any time. Earning a star or other award meant truly being prepared at all times for arrivals by land or by sea. As the 1920s progressed into the 1930s, automobiles could appear at almost any time, and before that, personnel could arrive via nearby boat landings or the train station.

A short account of an automobile visit to Pemaquid Light, published in August 1927, shows the scene that visitors to the light might encounter on a pleasant day when it was kept by the Robinsons and then their successors, the Elwells: "We go out to Pemaquid Light.…Here we stand under the giant fog-bell, play with the kittens in the grass; run into fifty summer people lounging on the bluffs, looking off to those waters, wherein I seem to see." The writer imagined seeing a shipwreck, many of which had taken place at Pemaquid Point.[79]

Leroy S. Elwell would be the last full-time keeper at Pemaquid. He was released from his post in 1934, when Pemaquid Point became the first automated light in Maine. Before he was removed from his post, Elwell rescued three teenagers caught in a storm, making some people even more concerned about automation and what might happen without the eyes, ears and arms of the keeper and any family he might have with him.

Automation would bring some lasting changes to Pemaquid, but it did not change the weather, the sea or the rocks. As explained in 1924, after describing the hazardous rock near the point that "runs like a battlement" along the shore, "when a southeaster churns up the sea, the 'Amphitheater' [of hazardous rocks near the river and bay] presents a struggle as furious as any that was ever staged in the arenas of Rome."[80] In this case, no one enjoyed the battle—not the spectators or the ships and sailors caught at sea. It could be a fight to the finish, and the finish might well be grim.

BRETON FISHERMAN'S PRAYER

Dear God, be good to me;
The sea is so wide
And my boat is so small,
Amen.

4

SHIPWRECKS AND OTHER DISASTERS

One of the earliest known shipwrecks near Pemaquid Point is perhaps the most mysterious, and it occurred long before the lighthouse was built. It highlights the dangerous nature of the seacoast at Pemaquid and the need for a light there, although even with a lighthouse, not all accidents could be avoided, which subsequent decades and centuries would prove.

Maine has the closest shoreline in what is now the United States to the coasts of Europe, and many early explorers and settlers came to the New World via the Maine coast. As noted, Pemaquid Point was settled in the early 1600s, creating one of the earliest Caucasian communities in North America. A new group of settlers with their belongings, including cattle, horses and other livestock and domestic animals, headed to the settlement in 1635 and reached the shore only to encounter great loss.

On August 15, 1685, the *Angel Gabriel* crashed at Pemaquid Point. The ship—a 240-ton galleon similar to the *Mayflower* but about eighteen feet longer[81]—had come from Bristol, England (though it made a stop in Milford Have, Wales), and was bound for the village of Pemaquid. The boat made it to its destination on August 14, but the next day, it was dashed on the rocks.[82]

The ship carried merchandise to the New World, as well as settlers and their belongings and livestock. The settlers included Ralph Blaisdell and his family and John Cogswell and his family, whose descendants would, centuries later, have plaques installed near the lighthouse.

A hurricane struck the coast on August 15 at roughly 6:30 a.m., and the *Angel Gabriel* was destroyed. Most of the one hundred or so passengers had debarked to spend the night on land, but their belongings and livestock,

High waves at Pemaquid. *Photo by Trudy Irene Scee.*

except for what they needed for their first night ashore, remained on board. The ship had anchored, but this and any other safety measures were to no avail. As one source described it, "The anchors failed to hold and the *Angel Gabriel* crashed high on the rocks," where the lighthouse now stands. One of the crew was killed, as were three or four passengers. Some of the cargo was salvaged before what remained of the ship sank.[83]

Richard Mather, the grandfather of the well-known Cotton Mather and the father of Increase Mather, wrote about the wreck in his journal. He had visited the ship twice in the past, having come to the New World at the same time aboard the *James*. He wrote that it was "a strong ship and well furnished with fourteen or sixteen pieces of ordnance." Most sources state that it was a sixteen-gun ship.[84]

Of the wreck, which he did not witness firsthand, Mather wrote, "The *Angel Gabriel*, being then at anchor at Pemaquid, was burst in pieces and cast away in this storm, and most of the cattle and other goods, with one seaman and three or four passengers, did also perish therein."[85] In the twentieth and twenty-first centuries, archaeologists and treasure hunters would search for its remains to no avail.

Although there were relatively few Caucasian ships and settlers in New England at the time, there were still other wrecks and deaths in that mighty

Pemaquid Point Lighthouse

High waves coming into the cove between the easterly and westerly points on the far end of the peninsula. The location of the lighthouse is just out of view. As a storm worsened, the cove could also be quite dangerous. *Photo by Trudy Irene Scee.*

storm of 1635. The *James* was farther southwest when the storm struck at the Isles of Shoals off the coast of what would become Maine. The captain tried to seek haven during the storm and dropped anchor. But here, too, it was useless, and the ship was swept away while the captain tried to keep ahead of danger as best he could. Near Piscataqua, "when the ship was less than a cable's length from the rocks, the wind swung around." There had been "no hope of rescue," when the wind suddenly changed, according to mid-twentieth-century maritime historian Edward Rowe Snow. All around them, the crew and passengers could see the wrecks of less fortunate vessels. The Mather family and the other one hundred or so passengers on the *James* made it to Boston a day later.[86]

Some of those who had traveled on the dashed *Angel Gabriel* would remain in the area. One story has it that one of the men, a Mr. Bailey, who had made the crossing and survived the shipwreck, wrote back to England about the trip and the horrors of the hurricane, describing events in such detail that his wife, who had planned to join him, was too afraid to make the trip after reading his letter. He, too, was too afraid to make the return crossing, and the two never saw each other again.[87]

Some accounts stated, as relayed in 1943 by Edward Snow, that some of those onboard the *Angel Gabriel* had fears for some time about the safety of the ship. They had seen "signs" along the way, so when the storm actually hit, they saw it as a confirmation of their "superstitions" or premonitions.

Other shipwrecks would occur in more modern times—and possibly some happened before 1635—and after the construction of the lighthouse at Pemaquid. Life at sea remained difficult and dangerous and—for most—monetarily unrewarding. One adage had it that "those who would go to sea for pleasure would go to Hell for pastime." And when a storm was rising, life at sea would have been hellish indeed. Lights like those at Pemaquid tried to protect the lives of those onboard, as well as the cargo of a ship and the ship itself, and sometimes, they did. At other times, they did not.

By the mid-1830s, on a good night, a ship's crew might see a number of lights along the Maine coast—often more than one at a time—and their various signals could orient them as to their location. In some places, a lightkeeper could see other lights. In the more dangerous areas, that was often true, located as they generally were high on the edges of the coast or the islands nearby or even in ocean harbors and in the largest rivers.

As Connie Scovill Small wrote after she and her husband moved to the Sequin Island light:

> *I loved being in the tower at sunset. When I took that lens cover off and the light flashed, I could begin counting from Portland to Pemaquid Point as almost simultaneously the lights came on—thirteen of them. It was like saying, "hello," "hello," "hello," "hello," all down the coast....We knew that they were trying to do the same thing we were, protecting navigation. For [t]hat was the whole sum and substance of our job, to keep the light going when it should, for there was someone out there who would be running for the light. If it wasn't in proper operating order or wasn't lit, there was trouble. The lights were lifelines to the sailors and navigators.*[88]

Sometimes those lifelines did indeed save lives. In other cases, they did not. The seas were dangerous and, in storms, took many lives over the years.

The *Bath Daily Times*, a local newspaper, described the hazards at Pemaquid in the aftermath of a deadly 1903 storm. As the paper saw it, "That part of the coast is rocky and very dangerous although well lighted. Pemaquid itself terminates in two points with a little cove between, the eastern one high and bold with a lighthouse on the summit, and the other long and low, terminating in a treacherous ledge. Between Boothbay Harbor

One of the commemorative plaques marking the 1635 wreck of the *Angel Gabriel*. Photo by *Trudy Irene Scee*.

and Pemaquid are a series of jagged points and rocky islands, and to the eastward Muscongus Bay is filled with islands and shoals."[89]

The paper noted that there was a light seven miles out to sea on Monhegan Island, as well as at Port Clyde and Franklin Point, and they, along with the lights at Sequin Island and the Ram Island at Boothbay Harbor, would also be visible in fair weather. But in a terrible storm, "all of these lights are of little use, and the buoys are absolutely invisible." And if one were to go into the water at Pemaquid—because of a shipwreck or being swept from the rocks—an undertow also presents dangers.

On May 4, 1891, a ship at sea near Pemaquid Point floundered. According to the lightkeeper's "Wreck Report" at 2:30 p.m. that day, the *Annie F. Collins*, a fourteen-year-old American schooner weighing about seventy tons and registered in New York, wrecked at Pemaquid Point. The ship had a crew of just three men, and they were all lost. The ship had been carrying paving stone as cargo. The lighthouse keeper at the time was the aforementioned Charles A. Dolliver, who would still be at the light two years later, when another shipwreck occurred. During the time of this wreck, the ship had about one hundred tons of cargo—its value unknown—and had $1,200 assigned as damages. The ship had "foundered instantly," and the cause of causality was assigned as "leaking and full of water." The wind had been blowing at about sixty miles per hour.[90] The seas had not been calm that day.

Little was said of the incident in following decades and indeed for over a century. Newspaper perusals perhaps explain why. The press often did not carry local news in the way it did decades later, and many newspapers were used primarily as venues for selling goods and conveying national news. And ships were common on the Maine coast—an accident had to be a tragedy to garner attention. In addition, the press did not initially know the connection between the May 4 shipwreck—if they knew of it at all—and what happened a few days later.

On May 6, the *Bath Daily Times* included two reports from Boothbay Harbor just down the coast from the Pemaquid Point lighthouse. Dated May 4, the first report noted that the revenue cutter *Woodbury* had arrived that night with a body on board. The vessel also brought in the dory that the man had been found floating in, which was painted pink both inside and out. The ship had come across the dory at about 3:50 p.m. around three miles southwest of Pemaquid Point.[91]

When the *Woodbury* came alongside the dory, it had had not one but two bodies inside it. The waves were rough, and both bodies were soon washed overboard. One of the bodies was recovered, while the other was not—at least not immediately. The "painter of the dory was cut short," the paper noted, "indicating that the two unfortunate occupants had cut loose from a wreck."[92]

On May 7, the *Bar Harbor Record*, also a small local newspaper but in this instance, one northeast of Pemaquid Point, carried essentially the same news but stated specifically that the *Woodbury* had arrived in Boothbay that Monday, "having on board the body of a yet unknown man which was found in a dory near Pemaquid Point light that afternoon." The seas had been "very heavy and one of the bodies was washed away before it could be secured."[93] Like a later shipwreck, some people survived an initial wreck only to die in or near a smaller craft while desperately seeking haven.

A May 6 report noted that the *Bath Daily Times* had been on hand when the lieutenant of the *Woodbury* called on the local coroner, one Mr. Moody, and excitement had spread through Boothbay as events unfolded. The officer stated that when his men had first come across the dory, they thought it was full of men at work fishing but soon realized their mistake. They could see that the dory was nearly full of water when they came close to it, "while two bodies lay in the bottom."[94]

And the paper noted the testimony that "when the Woodbury's crew attempted to hoist the drifting craft on board, the weight of water in it caused the dory to break in two and the bodies were precipitated into the sea. One was safely landed on deck, but the other sank and did not reappear."[95]

When the steamer made it into the harbor, everyone was invited to look at the dead man so his body could be identified. According to the paper, "He was apparently about 25 years old, 5 feet 6 inches tall, and had a considerable bruise on the side of the head." Moreover, as described by the mariners, the man who was lost "was a little taller, thin, light complexioned, and brown hair[ed]."[96]

No one could identify the men, and as it stood then, "the mystery surrounding is one which impresses itself strongly on every seaman and various theories have been advanced regarding it." The dory was not a fishing boat. The men who had been aboard the cutter thought it to be a tender attached to a "small coaster" and theorized that "the craft must have capsized, and these men hastily attempted to escape in this craft." There was no water nor provisions in the dory, supporting this idea, and the report noted that the seas had been high that Monday.

It was thought that the man whose body had been rescued had died that afternoon and that he had not died of starvation, as he was plump and seemingly healthy. It was assumed that the men had to leave their other vessel quickly and had perhaps "succumbed to the chilly air and the cold water in which they sat."[97] Hypothermia, a more modern term, might have been the cause of death.

On May 7, the newspaper reported that the body of the unknown man had been placed in "the tomb at Boothbay, the hope being that the story of the tragedy will reach some one who can tell the facts or bring some relative or friend to claim the remains." There had been no identifying personal property found on his body. "The mystery man continues a mystery still," the paper concluded.[98]

Four days later, the paper offered a solution to the mystery. On May 11, 1891, the *Bath Daily Times* ran a short article titled "A Possible Clue." According to the paper, a possible explanation had been found. It stated:

> *Word has been received that on the morning of the day the half-filled dory was found, a small schooner loaded with brick, started from Rockland. Up to date, no word of the vessel has been received, and though it is possible that she may have been blown to sea or some possible delay may have kept her out of port longer than expected, there is a growing conviction that this brick laden vessel is the one from which the two dead seamen came; that in the heavy wind she was either capsized or foundered, and that the two sailors alone escaped. Word has been sent to Rockland, and it is hoped that some one may be able to recognize the body, which is at present in the receiving tomb at Boothbay.*[99]

The second body had not yet been recovered, and according to lighthouse records, if this was indeed the same crew from the *Annie F. Collins*, three men had drowned in the shipwreck, but bodies were not always recovered from the sea then, as now.

As the keeper's report described the aftermath of the wreck—as well as can be deciphered from the script—on May 4 at 3:00 p.m., the "cutter *Woodbury* fell in with boat with two men [*sic*] in it, Pemaquid...they got the boat alongside the cutter and in trying to hoist her up the boat turned over and Capt. John l. Comb was...[tossed] out and...the body of...Thomas was [secured] and taken in to Boothbay. Boat was full of water when picked up." The note seems to have been dated June or July 1, 1893, and was signed by Jacob C. Crouck. This—as with the other notes—is difficult to decipher due to the aging and wear and tear on the document, and the ink used in the handwritten notes has faded in places. The edge of the form, where it is dated, is damaged.

Two of the bodies, it seems, had been identified over the course of a month or so, as had the owner of the ship, Edw. M. Coleman. Thomas may have been from England, and the third person who died was "unknown," with the number of deaths specified as "3 all told." The schooner had departed South Thomaston on May 2 for New York. And on the lightkeepers form, it was noted, "No assistance rendered." The note also stated, where asked if the ship was "over laden," "she was."[100] The wreck had not been witnessed by anyone, as far as can be determined.

Other people also drowned off the coast of Pemaquid due to ships sinking or wrecking—some on the rocks in front of the light or beyond or to the sides of them. In some cases, they knew the area was dangerous and were aware that the light was there for just that reason but went into trouble just the same.

Published in 1914, J. Henry Cartland's *Twenty Years at Pemaquid: Sketches of Its History and Remains*, which focused not on the light at Pemaquid but rather on the colonial settlement and its subsequent forts, gave one detailed account of an earlier drowning of a man, Mr. Henry Sproul, who had a boat moored nearby at Crow Island, where he lived with another man, Mr. Fred Partridge, both of whom were from Pemaquid Beach but were residing on the tiny island to catch lobsters. Their anchored boat filled with water after an easterly gale hit the vicinity. The mast and sail were blown away but not too far, and Sproul rowed out to try to rescue the sail. He had repeated problems, one being that the rowlock on the small boat came out a few times—the last time causing his boat to lean to one side and capsize. Sproul could not swim, and, wearing his heavy "oil clothes" and rubber boots, he quickly sank from the view of Mr. Partridge, who had been watching and tying to help him secure his property.[101]

The weather continued to worsen, with snow and heavy gales, and Partridge spent the night outside watching. At dawn, he built a fire and hoisted his blanket into a tree beside it and attracted the attention of two men on a nearby island. The men came to help Partridge, and they were eventually able to secure the body of the drowned Sproul with fishing hooks.[102]

Cartland continued in this vein, describing or noting that several people had drowned in the vicinity since his arrival in 1888, although it is unclear how close to the light they were or the exact causes of the drownings. The drowning of Charles Geyer, however, directly involved boats and the Pemaquid rocks. About fifty year earlier, as Cartland described it, dating the event to perhaps the 1860s, a "Captain of Pemaquid," Charles Geyer,

The other family memorial to the 1635 shipwreck of the *Angel Gabriel*. Photo by Trudy Irene Scee.

and two of his sons were returning to Portland with provisions he had purchased in the bigger port city—in exchange for fish caught earlier and reserved in a pickling mixture, it seems—when a severe storm hit them about three miles from home. They tried to continue, but near the passage into harbor (then called "the thread of life" by locals), just as they had almost made it home, the light no doubt helping them locate their position, a heavy wave hit their vessel, dashing it on the rocks and destroyed it. The three were able to make it into their "small boat" and survived the short distance to shore, but they lost everything else, including a violin Geyer had bought.[103]

Various drownings and mishaps occurred in the nineteenth century, as would be true in later years, and then, on September 18, 1893, the *Alice B. Higgins*, carrying paving stone, as had the *Annie F. Collins* in 1891, crashed on the rocks. Its crew members did manage to save themselves, rowing to shore by boat and landing near the lighthouse. The schooner, however, was lost.

A surviving report from the lightkeeper notes that the wind had been coming from the "S.S.W.," with a "moderate breeze, [and] Southerly Swells." The amount of insurance carried on the vessel and the cargo—

Left: The light at dusk in autumn. No matter the season or weather, the light goes on every night as the sun sets or as the cloud cover thickens. *Photo by Trudy Irene Scee.*

Below: The rocks that extend out into the Atlantic have presented a hazard to ships since before a lighthouse was built at Pemaquid Point. *Photo by Trudy Irene Scee.*

Above: The view from just below the ledge shows an arrangement of buildings remarkably unchanged since the 1890s. *Photo by Trudy Irene Scee.*

Left: The tower on a summer day is an appealing sight not to be missed. *Photo by Trudy Irene Scee.*

Right: Pemaquid Point Park in late spring. The lighthouse keeper's house almost blocks the view of the light from this angle, which is downhill from the tower. The white fence separates the keepers house and the tower from the rest of the park. *Photo by Trudy Irene Scee.*

Below: When standing on the rocks below the lighthouse, one may get a false sense of security. Although this exact position is relatively safe at low tide in calm weather, the situation can rapidly change. *Photo by Trudy Irene Scee.*

A side view taken outside of Lighthouse Park at Pemaquid during a storm. The cliffs or ledge plummeting into the sea are quite visible. *Photo by Trudy Irene Scee.*

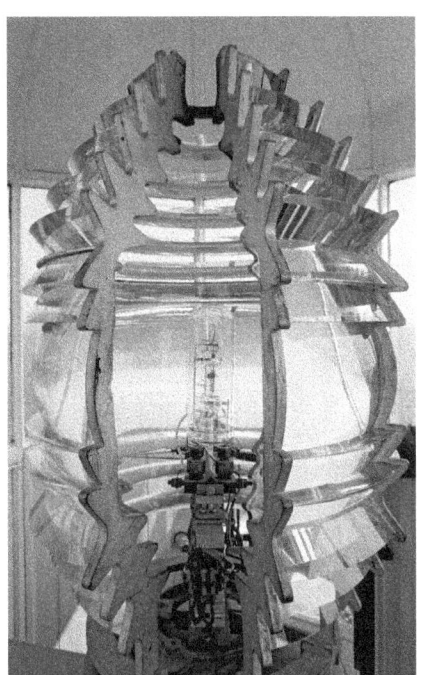

Above, left: A fourth order Fresnel lens on exhibit at Pemaquid Point's museum. *Photo by Trudy Irene Scee.*

Above, right: The Fresnel lens in the lantern room at Pemaquid Point. *Photo by Trudy Irene Scee.*

Right: The iron spiral staircase leading to the lantern room. The tower is accessible to the public via the Friends of the Pemaquid Point Lighthouse. *Photo by Trudy Irene Scee.*

Above: Just a little down the ledge, a rogue wave strikes the rocks. This is a constant potential danger, as people continue to get too close to the water, even after warnings. *Photo by Trudy Irene Scee.*

Left: The tower at Pemaquid Point as the sun had just started to sink and the light had just come on. A marvelous sight. *Photo by Trudy Irene Scee.*

Above: The tower just when a late season storm was about to begin. *Photo by Trudy Irene Scee.*

Right: The tower with its light on, viewed from the edge of the cliff. *Photo by Trudy Irene Scee.*

A side view of the lighthouse at sunset in autumn, including the tower and the keeper's house. *Photo by Trudy Irene Scee.*

The bell tower as a 2018 storm approaches. The crashing waves are visible beyond the building. *Photo by Trudy Irene Scee.*

This is the kind of weather in which no keeper wanted to see people climbing on the rocks. They might fear conditions would worsen over time, presenting hazardous conditions for people on the shore and ships on the ocean. *Photo by Trudy Irene Scee.*

The sun goes down on Pemaquid Point, 2018. *Photo by Trudy Irene Scee.*

The upstairs of the keeper's house is now available for rent, and some people claim that it is haunted. *Photo by Trudy Irene Scee.*

An autumn day at the lighthouse, autumn and even winter are very popular for visitors, although the lighthouse itself closes at the end of October. *Photo by Trudy Irene Scee.*

Top: The day ends. It is time for the visitors to leave the museum and the tower. *Photo by Trudy Irene Scee.*

Bottom: The view so many people come to Pemaquid to see—the light going on during a summer evening as the sun sets to the west. *Photo by Trudy Irene Scee.*

The Hotel Pemaquid, located just outside Pemaquid Park, has provided facilities to area visitors since 1888. *Photo by Trudy Irene Scee.*

The light in winter. *Photo by Trudy Irene Scee.*

Left: A near replica of the fog bell that once sent warnings to mariners near Pemaquid Point was donated by the Coast Guard and now sits in the side yard near the keeper's house. This is an actual fog bell and saw service elsewhere in days gone by. *Photo by Trudy Irene Scee.*

Below: Day closes. *Photo by Trudy Irene Scee.*

Top: Looking up from the point to the lighthouse. *Photo by Trudy Irene Scee.*

Bottom: Another view up from the rocks below. *Photo by Trudy Irene Scee.*

Top: The beauty of Pemaquid never disappoints the thousands of people who visit each year. *Photo by Trudy Irene Scee.*

Bottom: The bell house is locked to the public during the winter season yet continues to attract visitors, who examine the small replacement bell outside, look through its windows at the displays inside and wonder over its precarious position at the edge of the cliff. *Photo by Trudy Irene Scee.*

Left: Another view of the light tower and its entrance building from the "back" or ocean side. *Photo by Trudy Irene Scee.*

Below: The small cove between the "points" at Pemaquid Point, as seen on a fairly calm evening. *Photo by Trudy Irene Scee.*

which was deemed a total loss—was marked "unknown." According to the report, which seems to have directly quoted the captain, "The vessel commenced to crak [sic] when off Monhegan at 12:30 and I had to run her on to Pemaquid Point to save lives." It also stated, "After vessel struck the rocks at 2:20 pm, Schr. became a total wreck in two hours. We took to the boats, and landed at Pemaquid Light, afterwards coming to Boothbay Harbor, Me." The script of the account was signed by "John Berrio, Master" and dated September 19, 1893.[104]

The estimated value of the ship was $2,500 and its cargo, specified as paving stone, as $500. The vessel had sailed from Wellfleet, Massachusetts. It was twenty-six years old and, as indicated, under the charge of John Berrio. Noah S. Higgins owned the *Alice B. Higgins*, and resided in Wellfleet, Massachusetts. The ship had just sailed from Sullivan, Maine, with its cargo and had been headed to New York. According to later accounts, local residents went down to the rocks and gathered the granite paving stone that came in, finding it particularly valuable for foundation work.[105]

There was little notice of the incident in the press. The *Bath Daily Times* did mention it briefly. The paper simply noted a day later that "the schooner *Alice B. Higgins* from West Sullivan [headed] for New York sprang a leak and was beached on Pemaquid Point Monday, and is going to pieces. Her cargo of granite is insured and there is some insurance on the vessel."[106] Another incident, several years later, would be noted by the press up and down the state and elsewhere.

The worst, for many, was yet to come. During the night of September 17–18, 1903, a deadly storm, following tumultuous sea and wrecks and a few deaths up and down the East Coast, came to Pemaquid. That night, the sea claimed the lives of many, many men at Pemaquid Point.

But before that, a little-known accident would occur off Pemaquid Point. On November 26, 1898, a monstrous storm and blizzard hit coastal New England.

On display at the Fisherman's Museum, this ship's binnacle has been preserved long after it aided its captains in the storms. *Photo by Trudy Irene Scee.*

The storm is most known for the shipwreck of the steamer *City of Portland*, which was built in 1889 as a ferry between Boston and Portland. More than two hundred people died as the steamer tried to reach Portland from Boston. Altogether, more than four hundred people died during the blizzard. At Pemaquid Point, a ship met near disaster, and its ultimate fate went unknown for over a week.[107]

At Pemaquid, as described by J. Henry Cartland, "the schooner *H.H. Chamberlain*, with four young men aboard, was blown out of the harbor and away south to the Gulf Stream." The Pemaquid Point Light may have alerted the captain to his ship's exact location, but although he avoided crashing on the point, his vessel was feared lost after being tossed on the heavy seas away from its destination.[108]

Starting on November 28, the local papers covered the storm with great detail for the times. The *Bath Times* did so, as did others. Front-page headlines were a relatively new thing in 1898, but the Bath paper—like others in the state—used them.

The day after the storm broke, the local paper announced, "Results of the Storm: Many Vessels Wrecked. Feared that Barges *Virginia* and *Lucy A. Nickels* Are Lost." In addition, a schooner sailing from Deer Island, not so far from Pemaquid, had wrecked at Fresh Island, and the captain and his son perished after encountering the storm near Cape Ann, which is where the *City of Portland* sank in the same storm. Two other crew members managed to reach an island from which they were rescued.[109]

On the inside pages, the paper reported on "The Storm in Bath." The coverage perhaps explains why there was no immediate communication with Pemaquid. The paper stated, "The terrific blizzard which swept over New England yesterday struck Bath with full force, blocking the streets and sidewalks with immense drifts, stopping all progress on the electric road and cutting off communication by mail and telegraph." Pemaquid, being more isolated, may also have been hard hit and perhaps blocked from outside communication.

Ships in the Kennebec River, which runs into the ocean at Bath, were torn loose from moorings. Some ships moored at the coastline were damaged, and the schooner *Ben Hur* broke its chains at Five Islands and went ashore at Dry Point.[110] More dire reports followed.

November 29 came with the news of the wreck of the steamer *Portland*. Thirty-four bodies had washed ashore already, as had pieces of luggage and debris. The full death count would never be known, as the only passenger lists went down with the ship, but estimates go to up to 250 dead. Other wrecks were also included in the paper that day. A front-page article stated, as wired from Boston, that so much damage from a storm had not been seen in or near the Boston Harbor "since Minot's light was carried away in 1851," thus bringing lighthouses back into the story and the danger Pemaquid Lighthouse's first keeper had tried to warn the authorities about.[111]

Highlighting, perhaps, part of the situation surrounding the fate of the ship that was forced to sea from Pemaquid, the article noted that although it was generally thought that a ship with "strong ground tackle out is safe from any storm," at least in that Boston harbor, the theory had been proved wrong when "a dozen vessels dragged their anchors, even in that haven [the upper harbor] and were dashed against the wharves or into one another." Bringing the Pemaquid region directly into the coverage, the Boston article reported that "there is scarcely a bay, harbor, or inlet from the Penobscot to New London [Connecticut] that has not on its shores the bones of some craft." In addition, navigation buoys had been knocked out of position. Another article in the local paper covered the wreck of a Bath schooner that had left the Kennebec and sank at Vineyard Haven. The captain perished, but a few of his men were saved. The paper lamented the death of Captain Roberts, a respected local man. News of deaths of other locals would arrive in subsequent days.[112]

The next day came with the news of thirty more wrecks along the New England coastline. Anyone awaiting news of the *H.H. Chamberlain*, which had disappeared from Pemaquid, would have had much searching to do to find news. In addition, a new storm swept down the coast, causing further difficulties. Some points had still not been heard from regarding wrecks and fatalities from November 28.[113]

It was not until December 6 that the paper devoted a short article—actually a long paragraph—to the fate of the *Henry H. Chamberlain*. On that day, the paper noted that the ship had, rather involuntarily, left from Pemaquid with a supply of oil and factory supplies. "She was anchored in Pemaquid Harbor when the violent gale of November 27 burst upon her," the *Times* reported. Owned by F.S. Bowker of Philipsburg, the ship was under the authority of Captain Fossett of Round Pond when caught in the storm.[114]

The heavy seas had tossed the ship, "dragged" it "on a ledge and was pounding heavily, when the captain ordered her port chain, kedge, and hawser slipped and the vessel put to sea, encountering a terrific gale, but escaping with loss of foretopsail and yawl boat." The ship's captain in this misadventure clearly knew where he was when the storm started, so the light at Pemaquid, in that regard, was perhaps not of great help, though it may have helped the captain steer his ship away from the point and aim it as best as possible to safety elsewhere.[115]

At some point in the crew's harry journey, the captain was able to procure another anchor, and the ship proceeded to New York. As the Bath paper described it on December 6, 1898, "the schooner *Henry H. Chamberlain* arrived in Vineyard Haven on Saturday after an exciting passage."[116] That was the same location where a Bath schooner sank just days earlier.

Other storms would cause problems along the coast near Pemaquid in subsequent years, and then in the early 1900s, calamity would ensue. As described by the press, on a deadly night in 1903, according to the *Bangor Daily Commercial* (*BDC*), "Two vessels were wrecked on the treacherous bar at the end of Pemaquid Point and 15 hardy mariners went down to their deaths." The vessels that wrecked that night were a mackerel seiner (a rugged schooner); the *George L. Edmunds*, owned by Captain Willard G. Poole of Gloucester, Massachusetts, who also commanded the ship; and a smaller vessel, a coasting schooner, the *Sadie and Lillie*, under Captain Harding of Machias, Maine. The *Sadie and Lillie* had hailed from Machias, was built in Steuben, Maine, in 1884, and measured sixty-four by twenty-three feet and was a two-masted schooner. It was headed from Prospect to Boston when caught in the storm.

As increasing winds and darkening skies had given warning of a storm about to break, the captains of both ships had sought to bring their ships to safe harbor, as both had been sailing "well off shore" when signs of the impending storm set in. Night closed in quickly under ominous clouds, and the vessels were tossed in the treacherous seas long before they reached safe haven. Punishing rains fell, blocking all but fleeting sights of the lights along the shore, as did the height of the waves. Captain Harding chose to go to Sequin Light to seek refuge in the broad mouth of the Kennebec River, but in the worsening conditions, he went to Pemaquid instead, mistaking which light he was able to see from time to time. His ship was ultimately "dashed on the rocky point at Pemaquid."[117]

A "volunteer life saver," Weston Curtis, after much struggling, was able to pull two of Harding's men to safety after succeeding in getting a line out to the *Sadie and Lillie*. While Curtis was trying to get the line to the vessel, Harding had been trying to secure the boat in a safer position. He was the last on the boat to try to reach safety on the shore, but by then, conditions had worsened, and the line had become twisted after the rescue of the two crewmen. When Harding was about halfway to shore, the line stuck, and Curtis drowned as the men on the shore looked on

Another view of the bell tower. *Photo by Trudy Irene Scee.*

helplessly. His body was recovered, but it was thought that his schooner would be a total loss.[118]

Meanwhile, sixteen men had been aboard the *Edmunds*. Fourteen of them, including Captain Poole, perished in the storm. Captain Poole had tried to round the point but crashed ashore on the eastern side of the point before he could do so. He was able to reach the western side of the point but thought his ship would not survive the gale on that side, as it was more exposed. So, he tried to round the point. By this time, according to the coverage of the wrecks, the winds had reached almost hurricane speed, and the vessel crashed on the rocks. Fishing vessels like this were thought by many—according to the local press—to be able to weather almost any storm, but the *Edmunds* did not survive the night.

The men aboard, as the press reported, put "dory after dory" over the side of the wrecked ship to try to reach the shore, but each, in turn, was dashed on the rocks. Finally, one of the small boats was able to get away from the ship, but after it was about halfway through the hazardous waters, it capsized with five men aboard who then struggled to survive in the "boiling sea." Two of the men, although deemed "more dead than alive," did manage to reach safety. The other fourteen men who had been on the ship died, including Captain Poole.[119] It would later be revealed that the two survivors had each managed to grab a toehold on the rocks and pulled themselves in, but neither knew that other was alive until the dawn broke the next morning.

The following morning, the *Bangor Daily News* ran the headline "SCORES OF MEN AND SHIPS LOST IN THE TERRIBLE STORM; Two Schooners Wrecked Off Pemaquid Point—Fifteen of the Nineteen Men Aboard Were Drowned, Captain Harding of Prospect Lost." And, as the subheading continued, "Steamer Mexicana Founders with All on Board Lost Save One—Long List of Disasters All Along the Coast."[120]

In terms of the disasters near the Pemaquid Light, the *Bangor Daily News* stated that "both wrecks resulted from the sailing masters miscalculating their positions in the thick weather. Captain Poole thought he was making Boothbay Harbor [not too distant] while Captain Harding believed his course was leading him into the Kennebec Harbor nearly forty miles from Pemaquid." The paper also reported, "When the two ships went on the ledges they were less than 200 yards apart."[121] That closeness alone—were they on the same side of the point in front of the lighthouse—could have proved perilous in inclement weather near the Pemaquid rocks.

Both ship captains had been far off the coastline, and both had headed for safe harbor when the increasing gales and thickening clouds gave warning

Headlines from the *Bangor Daily News* after the 1903 wrecks at Pemaquid. *Photo by Trudy Irene Scee.*

of a great storm approaching. The newspapers repeated reports of the storm and said that both ships were still far from safety when it burst on them. Moreover, "the beacon lights which blinked faintly through sheets of rain when they momentarily appeared above the crests of the mountainous waves, gave but little assistance." Captain Harding perhaps lost his life due to this, as "he chose Sequin, but in the thick weather picked up Pemaquid light and instead of finding safety in the broad Kennebec his vessel was dashed on the rocky point at Pemaquid."[122]

The *Bangor Daily News* used reports from Pemaquid, based at least partly on interviews with four surviving crew and with Weston Curtis, who the newspaper said had witnessed the wreck, and who, with Harding's men, had watched the captain die as the line was caught. The ships had been dashed to pieces, and "their timbers were strewn over hundreds of yards of the shore line."

Many of the crew of the two ships had been from Massachusetts and Maine, while a few came from the Canadian Maritimes and elsewhere. That Wednesday night into Thursday, three bodies were recovered, including

Headlines from the *Bangor Daily News* after the 1903 wrecks at Pemaquid. These focus on shipwrecks in other locations. *Photo by Trudy Irene Scee.*

Captain Poole's. Initially, only Captain Harding's body was recovered, but after some time, the two other bodies washed ashore.

As identified in the *Bangor Daily News*, with much of it also contained in various reports, including those of the lightkeeper, nine of the deceased men from the *George L. Edmunds* had come from Massachusetts, most from Gloucester and two from New Brunswick. Of the dead of the *Sadie and Lillie*, the captain was from Prospect, Maine, and left behind three children, and the two men saved were from Verona and Belfast, Maine. From the *Edmunds*, those saved were from Nova Scotia and Massachusetts. Of the two other men—in addition to Captain Harding—whose bodies had been recovered, both were from Gloucester. One left behind a wife and three children, and the other left behind a wife.

A report from Gloucester published September 18 in the *Boston Journal* was titled "Woe in Gloucester Over Loss of *Edmunds*." The article stated, "Fifteen dead out of a crew of eighteen, and the wreck of a staunch Schooner, the *George F. Edmunds*, were the tidings which cast dismay among Gloucester men today. Shortly before 1 o'clock this morning the vessel went ashore at Pemaquid Point, Me., and Captain Willard G. Poole and thirteen out of his crew of fifteen were lost. Knowledge of the vessel's loss came through press dispatched, and caused the wildest excitement. The captain was exceptionally popular, and every member of the crew was known to all seafaring men."[123]

As the names of those few who survived the fishing wreck were unknown for some time, everyone feared the worst, and most who had loved ones on the ships would learn the worst. The men had set out just three weeks before the wreck on what had been the third-largest ship sailing from that port. Built in 1887, the ship was insured with the China Mutual Insurance Company.[124]

Three more bodies were recovered during the night following the wrecks—all three identified and all three from the *Edmunds*. "Watchers," however, had stayed on the lookout all night and "saw several bodies washing about in the surf, but the tide was running so high that no attempt could be made to recover them. It is believed that they will come ashore during the day,"[125] the press stated.

Moreover, the paper reported, "The four survivors of the disaster still remain here to look after their dead shipmates. They probably will return home Saturday and it is expected the bodies recovered will be sent home at that time."[126]

The Town of Bristol would later report the names of all of the dead in its annual report of 1904 and would note the expenses incurred by the wreck. The costs highlighted the devastation brought by the storm. They included undertaker bills, cots and supplies for the undertakers in the days following the shipwrecks, grave digger's expenses and the hiring of horses and rooms in houses. Some of the expenses were reimbursed by Gloucester, and a little from Prudential Life, but retrieving and burying the dead still cost the town $168—not an insignificant amount at the time.

The lightkeeper, too, filled out a form briefly describing the event and listing the men involved. Keeper Clarence E. Marr's wreck report listed the *George F. Edmunds* as a sixteen-year-old American schooner registered as vessel number 8595 at port in Gloucester, Massachusetts, with Willard Poole designated as both the ship's master and its owner. The ship was headed to Maine with no passengers—only the captain and the fifteen-person crew. The names of the dead were listed, and the fact that the ship had no deck load was noted. The ship was a "total loss," the report stated, and it identified the precise location of the wreck as "about 100 rods west of Pemaquid light." The "nature of the casualty" was listed as "stranded." The new information, as recorded, was that "one of the crew saved says Capt, judged his vessel 5 miles from the light and was going into Johns Bay. Clear at time of passing

Pemaquid Point Lighthouse

The rocks in the rain. *Photo by Trudy Irene Scee.*

The storm during the 1903 blizzard caused waves much higher and deadlier than these. *Photo by Trudy Irene Scee.*

light. Rain and wind came up suddenly." Frank Drummund, it seems, dated the report September 22, 1903.

The local newspaper also attempted to describe the situation with the headline "At Pemaquid, Two Schooners Wrecked Near the Light Last Night. Fifteen Lives Lost in Disaster. In the Gale and Mist They Lost Their Bearings, One Striking the West and the Other the East Point." It carried a press release from Damariscotta, but special to the *Bath Daily Times*, the paper stated, "In the terrible gale of last night, when the wind was blowing fifty or sixty miles an hour and the sea dashing high on the ragged rocks of that part of the coast and the rain driven before the hurricane made it impossible to see even the lights, two schooners…were wrecked on Pemaquid Point and fifteen of their crews were drowned, including both of the captains."[127]

The *Times* described the double points at Pemaquid Point and noted that the lights that would have been visible in good weather were likely of little use in the huge storm that had just hit the coast. It surmised that "the schooners were probably trying to make Boothbay for shelter when they were dashed on the cruel rocks at Pemaquid."[128]

In a separate insert, the paper noted, "Capt. J.S. Poole who commanded the Gloucester mackerel seiner that wrecked last night at Pemaquid Beach was well known in this city. He went down with his vessel."[129]

The shipwrecks at Pemaquid were not the only casualties of the storm, though. A *Portland Press* article, much like the *Bangor Dailey News* coverage, called it "a storm of such intensity that its parallel is not recorded in the local weather bureau's statistics for any previous September." The storm "swept along the coast of Maine early Thursday, leaving death and destruction in its wake," the paper noted, stating that so far, only the fatalities and total shipwrecks at Pemaquid had been reported, but dozens of other boats were seriously damaged, trees were uprooted along the coast and crops in the path of the storm were destroyed. The paper credited Weston Curtis for saving the two men he had rescued singlehandedly and stated that Captain Poole's final trip was scheduled to be his last journey at sea; he had planned to retire when his ship pulled back into port. Moreover, he had died only a few miles from his birthplace.[130]

As the *Bangor Daily News* noted in its separate coverage, other wrecks and casualties had occurred along the coastline. A yacht was wrecked off Richmond's Island. The four men aboard were able to save themselves and reached Portland eventually, and on September 19, a short article from Manchester, Massachusetts, identified the owner and stated that the yacht had been thrown against the rocks at the breakwater in the hurricane-force

Pemaquid Point Lighthouse

Left: For whom the bell tolled. One caregiver would hear it toll for him, and he would die at the place he had loved. *Photo by Trudy Irene Scee.*

Below: The waves have washed up bodies at the base of the lighthouse for centuries. *Photo by Trudy Irene Scee.*

Pemaquid Point Lighthouse

The view from the lantern room down over the bell tower, the rocks and the ocean. *Photo by Trudy Irene Scee.*

gales. The men were able to climb up the granite boulders with much difficulty and managed to survive after crawling to safety.[131]

On Tuesday, September 15, when the storm was just starting to head up the coast in Florida, the steamship *Mexican* floundered and of its crew of twenty-two, all but one perished. The lone survivor had held onto a piece of the wreckage until a British steamer rescued him.[132]

All along the Eastern Seaboard during the next few days, ships had wrecked. A dory capsized just off the Boston Light, and four Swedish men were rescued clinging to the rigging by ships returning from Maine and by a local tugboat.[133]

Coverage of the storm had actually started the day before the storm hit Maine. On September 17, when several marine disasters occurred south of Maine, the *Bangor Daily News* ran the headline "Many Disasters on the Delaware Coast: Schooner *Hattie A. Marsh* with Stone from Maine Dashed to Pieces—Captain and Four of Crew Drowned—Three Barges and Their Crews Lost." Moreover, the president of the United States Theodore Roosevelt had witnessed a tug towing a large schooner sink. The storm had been working its way up the coast when it hit the Delaware capes, where it raged for four hours with winds up to eighty miles per hour and rain "falling in torrents."[134]

The schooner *Hattie A. Marsh* had been coming from Painter's Point, Maine, and was headed for Philadelphia with a cargo of paving stones, much like the ships sunk off Pemaquid Point a few years earlier. The captain had tried to reach the harbor but, unable to do so, was forced to drop anchor. The anchor did not hold, and the ship "was dashed on the rocks of the harbor of rescue." A steamer tried to save the men but could only rescue two. Four others, including the captain, drowned.[135]

Not far away from the *Hattie A. Marsh*, three schooners dragging their anchors collided. One of them sank, and the others sustained severe damage. A light in the region was carried away and offered no further guidance in its vicinity.

Reports came in from New York that on September 15, the region had been visited "by the fiercest wind and rain storm known hereabout in years." Thousands of dollars in damages had been sustained. Farther north, a ship crashed in the New Haven, Connecticut harbor. In many coastal areas, falling trees and other destruction cut off telephone and telegraph communication. Some houses were destroyed, and many ships were forced to find harbor or face destruction.[136]

This was the storm that blew up the coast of Maine and wrecked the ships at Pemaquid. But they were not the only ones in Maine to suffer in the storm. Not far to the east or northeast from Pemaquid, a three-mast schooner floundered off the coast of Mount Desert Island—home to the Bass Harbor Lighthouse—about twenty miles out to sea. The Spartan had left Windsor, Nova Scotia, for New York the previous Saturday, when it encountered the storm southeast of Mount Desert. The ship, heavily loaded with "plaster rock," sprang a leak, and the high waves crashing over the deck disabled its gasoline-powered pumps. At about 10:00 p.m., the vessel had eight feet of water in its hold.

The captain was determined to stay with the ship, hoping it would not sink. Then the mizzen mast, followed by the main mast, flew overboard. The storm continued, the ship seemed in danger of being totally submerged and the captain finally had a small boat lowered over the side with his wife and daughter the first aboard. Eleven people managed to get in the boat and get away from the danger of the injured schooner at about 11:00 p.m., and the group left in the high seas, headed for what they hoped was the shore. Four hours later, the schooner *Arcadia* sighted the boat and managed to pull everyone onboard. Although salvage attempts were made, only a few instruments were saved. The ship had been built in Bath, Maine, in 1880. Its value was estimated at $20,000, and it was uninsured. Its cargo, worth $3,000, was insured.[137]

A little farther to the north and east, the schooner *Yreka* went ashore at Schoodic Point and crashed on the rocks. The fog had been dense, and the schooner from nearby Ellsworth was returning from Boston and had encountered gale-force winds. The crew had managed to stay the ship for eight hours through the night of September 17, even after loosing the foremast head, and then the crippled ship ran on Schoodic Point. The crew was able to "jump" onto the rocks near the point to safety. Had the ship gone down earlier in the night, when it was farther out, it was believed that all would have perished. Within ten minutes of their leaving the schooner, the captain reported, "There was not a piece of the schooner left as large as a trunk." The captain had tried to go back to rescue some things from his cabin and was nearly killed doing so. The vessel was uninsured.[138]

For days after this deadly storm, people continued to wait for bodies to wash up or be otherwise recovered. Three more bodies were recovered of the missing by the night following the wrecks, bringing the number of the bodies recovered to six. The seas remained rough, though, and some ships that tried to leave Maine harbors were forced to return.[139]

The rescued men stayed at Pemaquid for a few days after the wrecks to look after the bodies of their crew. They were expected to leave that

Saturday, though. Captain Harding's funeral was held on September 18, and his body was taken to Prospect for burial. He died only about three miles from his birthplace.[140]

While all of this was going on, another storm hit the region. Thursday night, a storm judged almost as bad as the first one raged for several hours. What little remained of the wrecked ships was further destroyed, and as the report from Pemaquid that Friday stated, "Friday nothing remained of the big fisherman, *George L. Edmunds*, and the spot where the little coaster Sadie and Lillie met her fate, was marked only by a battered and broken piece of the hull tossing among the rocks."[141]

On September 23, reports came in from Boothbay Harbor, stating that five bodies from the *George F. Edmunds* had washed ashore late on Thursday. Horace Taylor was identified from a ring in his vest pocket, where he also had $22.65, perhaps put there when he knew his chances for survival were slim or that the ship might not make it. By late that Thursday, eight bodies were recovered and seven were still missing.[142] Some of them may have been those spotted off Pemaquid late on the Thursday night after the wrecks—ones that the bystanders could not retrieve in the dangerous seas.

A later report stated that one of the two survivors of the *Edmunds* had heard the sound of the ship breaking apart "and the horrible screams that followed, but only a few minutes of that dreadful sea were needed to smother every groan." And then the bodies had started to come ashore.[143]

And then came the funerals. Some, and perhaps all, of the funerals were held together, at least the ones held at Pemaquid. Other services may have been held in the men's hometowns, especially for those who lived farther away. One report stated, "Still more heart rendering" than the screams that some had heard the night of the shipwreck and the sounds of the ships breaking apart "was the funeral of the victims, held in a summer cottage a day later. The note of the waves mingled with the voices of those who spoke the last words over the victims of the unaccountable veil that dimmed the light that dreadful night."[144]

According to a 1914 report, the body of Captain Willard Pool was found the following spring. John Lewis, who had been saved from the shipwrecks, died the next winter from the cold, perhaps hypothermia, in Boston Bay, "while in an open dory on a fishing trip." He had told people after the wrecks off Pemaquid that it had been his sixth close call and that the next one would kill him. It did. As the author of the report stated, referring to Pemaquid itself, "Many vessels and hardy sailors have ended their career in this vicinity since the old *Archangel* perished here in 1635," the first known European ship to be "cast away on the New England Coast."[145]

Mariners were still, obviously, in need of further guidance along the Maine coast. Another light was being constructed, Ram Island Ledge. It was now, however, suspended for the season. About half of the work was finished, and its completion was expected for early autumn 1904.[146] Meanwhile, with the funerals over, the survivors soon left the area, although it was still hoped that more of the bodies might be recovered.

Sadly, one of the people who had interviewed the survivors after the wrecks, William P. Sawyer, would, forty-two years later, wash up at Pemaquid Point. His body was found near the lighthouse. No note or other indication was found to indicate why he died, and although his death is often shrouded in mystery, if noted at all, his would also be a tragic death.

Before Sawyer's death, a few years after the 1903 shipwrecks, a strong swimmer tempted the dangers of Pemaquid. The woman purportedly decided to have a soak in a natural bathing tub created by seawater being caught in one of the rock formations. The sea, however, was not complacent and soon crashed over the rocks, sweeping her out into the ocean. She was able to keep close enough to shore for a rescue but far enough out to avoid being crushed on the rocks. In the fog and the waves, she managed to stay afloat until a boat, directed by watchers and signals from the lighthouse and the keeper, rescued her.[147]

On August 17, 1917, the coastal schooner *Willis and Guy* crashed on the Pemaquid rocks in heavy fog. The crew of three was saved, but before the ship could be brought to safety, a hurricane hit, breaking it up four days later. The schooner had been carrying 216 tons of coal, and the ship and coal were scattered over the rocks. Area townspeople salvaged much of the coal for their own use, enough, it has been said, to heat their homes for the following winter. One of the locals stated that his father had gathered fifteen tons of coal and sold three of them.[148]

The *Bath Daily Times* quipped in its headline, "New Harbor and Also Pemaquid Have Now Plenty of Good Coal." Its special dispatch from New Harbor recounted the situation there. According to the *Times*, "Scores of people in this town and Pemaquid now have a generous supply of anthracite coal on hand, as a result of the breaking up of the schooner *Willis and Guy*." A "great undertow" had thrown the coal up on the shore, and the people from the two small communities "got busy gathering the harvest."[149]

At one point "during the height of the 'prospecting,' seventy-five people were engaged picking up coal. Sacks, baskets, and pails were used and as fast as filled were dumped into the owner's pile back from the water's edge to be hauled away later." An estimated one hundred tons of coal had come ashore.[150]

Locals benefited from the coal that washed up in 1917, but they often aided in rescues, too, or watched them and other events at Pemaquid and the immediate vicinity. Those at sea often benefited from the presence of locals. It was simply an odd twist when the locals benefited in such a direct manner. And they would benefit again a few years later, although in this case, it would be two summer families who received the primary benefit, as three of their members were rescued by the keeper, although other locals helped once again. But before that, another keeper went into the waves to save lives.

Herbert Robinson was sixty-eight years old in November 1927 and was about to retire when he rescued two people. An eighteen-year-old young man had been washed off the rocks near the lighthouse in rough seas and drowned. His uncle and aunt were also swept off the rocks, and Robinson went in after them. He rescued the couple at great risk to himself and was commended for his bravery. He had no chance to save the young man, as his body was not seen again after being washed into the ocean.[151]

Before automation came to Pemaquid, the last full-time keeper at Pemaquid Point, Leroy S. Elwell, risked his life to save those of three young people just a few years later. And then he almost lost them all, and himself, on the rocks.

A storm hit the coast of Maine on August 7, 1930. Before it hit, three high school students from Springfield, Massachusetts, had set out from Round Point, where Chester Neal Jr. and his fifteen-year-old sister, Barbara, were living in their family's summer home. Eighteen-year-old Betty Carlton was visiting for the day. The three headed to Pemaquid Point in a catboat—a small sailing craft—so that Betty Carlton could return to the home of Dr. James Commins, where she was staying.[152]

The seas were rough and choppy, according to a later report by the government, when a fierce squall hit the catboat and overturned it. The catboat quickly sank, leaving the three teens swimming as best as they could in the rough ocean waters.[153]

Elwell made repeated attempts in a small skiff before he finally reached the three weary teens. Then, after he was able to get them safely out of the high waves and into his skiff, the heavy seas "made landing impossible," and "calls for aid brought W.J. Burnside of Pemaquid and also a boat sent by Capt. Thomas Bracket of New Harbor," according to a 1930 release by the U.S. secretary of commerce.[154]

The secretary of commerce presented Elwell with a commendation on October 11, 1930, for his "rescue from drowning" of the three teens. Furthermore, "in announcing this honor," the press release stated, "the lighthouse service of the federal department of commerce explains that only outstanding acts of bravery receive this particular form of commendation."[155] The last keeper of the light had served his station and his community honorably.

Other storms would hit the Maine coast in following years. In November 1938, a calamitous storm—as bad as any of the previous years—hit New England. Fortunately, the storm did not spend its might on Maine and the Pemaquid area. Damage was not extensive in the region, although there were shipwrecks up and down the East Coast. The has been referred to as the Great Hurricane of 1938.

But on September 17, 1945, a heavily damaged body washed up on the rocks near the lighthouse. The gruesome discovery immediately came to the attention of the authorities. It turned out to be the body of William P. Sawyer. Sawyer had seen the events of the hurricane of 1903 and the wrecks at Pemaquid and had been on the beach when the bodies started to be recovered. Although at least one person immediately thought that it was Sawyer, the body required autopsy for official identification and cause of death.

Discovered almost exactly forty-two years after wrecks of the *George F. Edmunds* and the *Sadie and Lillie*, the body was sent to Dr. Joseph E. Porter for examination. Described as "virtually headless" by the *Bath Daily Times* report from New Harbor on September 18, the paper, nevertheless, had a lead.[156]

The *Bangor Daily News*, like other papers, reported on the discovery. It broke the story on September 17, with the subhead "Find Body in Sea, May Be Foul Play," and stated that, as sent in by the Associated Press on September 16 from New Harbor, "The body of an elderly man was found today washed ashore near Pemaquid Point lighthouse and authorities sought to learn his identity and the circumstances of his death."

Medical examiner Dr. J.G. Odlorne said the man, who was about sixty years old at death, had suffered a serious head injury and several bad body bruises and was dead before he reached the water.[157] Moreover, "Odlorne estimated the body had been in the sea two or three weeks."[158]

Arthur Lawson of Pemaquid Point settlement discovered the body on the morning of September 16. The body had been dressed in sneakers, a blue sweater and a white sweatshirt. His heavily tanned body suggested that he might have been "a seaman or a fisherman." He also "had gray

Pemaquid Point Lighthouse

hair and a moustache." The Maine State Police and the Lincoln County Sherriff's Office investigated.[159]

When the Bath newspaper reported the next day, it proclaimed right away, "Body Believed to Be That of W.P. Sawyer of Pemaquid." It stated that Portland pathologist Dr. Porter was examining the body, as authorities had been "puzzled by the condition of a man they were almost certain was William P. Sawyer, 66-year old Harvard Law School classmate of Franklin D. Roosevelt."[160]

The body had "drifted ashore Sunday near Pemaquid Point lighthouse, where Sawyer was caretaker." A local cousin and a friend were able to identify the body, the *Bath Daily Times* reported, as well as the clothing, and "a key tied to a vest fitted the lighthouse door." The clothing seems to have been a bit different than reported by the *Bangor Daily News*, though, and the description was a bit more gruesome.[161]

County attorney Charles M. Giles stated that everything at the lighthouse had been found in "careful order." The last entry in the lighthouse ledger was "15-cent charges for parking on the lighthouse reservation." It was dated September 13 (hence the body was not in the ocean for weeks), and said, "Money in secret drawer, $52.74," providing an interesting look at lighthouse and park operations. The secret drawer, however, was a simple drawer "in the lower part of a table and which anyone intent on robbing the caretaker could have discovered."[162]

Sawyer's cousin and the other person who identified the body said that there had been "a gun in the lighthouse several weeks ago but that a search [by the authorities] had failed to produce one." As medical examiner Odlorne had stated that the cause of death was unknown, Dr. Porter would perform an autopsy. Odlorne did confirm, however, that the man was "apparently 'dead before he reached the water.'" Sawyer had been a summer resident of Pemaquid Point since his childhood and had lived there permanently for about the previous fifteen years.

The following day, the newspapers confirmed Sawyer's identity. He was identified, too, as "a bachelor and one-time Boston lawyer," a "Harvard graduate and friend of Franklin D. Roosevelt." Although the papers did not point it out, Sawyer's friend, the former president, had died on April 12 of a cerebral hemorrhage after a long struggle with his health. To date, "the supposed death weapon, a gun missing from the Pemaquid Point lighthouse…had not been found."[163]

The next day, the *Bangor Daily News* stated that the death had been ruled a "suicidal shot in the head." The body had been only partially clad, but other clothing items had been found on September 18, aiding in the identification. The body was also specified as having been found about four hundred yards from the cliff at the point. The next day, the paper reported that the gun had still not been found, but that it could have "been carried away by the sea."[164] So ended the life of a person who loved Pemaquid Point and the lighthouse, was there during one of its worst disasters and had taken care to leave things in order and the doors locked before he departed the world, leaving just months after his friend, the president, left it.

5

PEMAQUID POINT LIGHTHOUSE

ITS PHYSICAL STRUCTURE, PERSONNEL AND EVENTS AFTER AUTOMATION

In 1934, Pemaquid Point found itself the center of much attention. The federal government was considering automating the station, and some locals did not want this, as, among other things, it would likely lead to the end of the lightkeeper's job at Pemaquid. Some people feared that the station might not be automated but abandoned altogether and the land sold to the highest bidder. The light had been at the point for more than one hundred years; had seen friendly visits, disasters and rescues; and had become a popular tourist destination. People were concerned about its fate and the repercussions for the community.

Concerns had started when—if not before—the commissioner of lights announced in May 1933 that seventeen lighthouse stations in Maine were to be discontinued or equipped with automatic controls as part of a national program to economize spending. Eight stations had already received notification of federal plans, two of which had already seen some changes, while another nine were on a list waiting for authorization. It was anticipated that by the close of June, the original eight would be either discontinued or automated, with the other nine undergoing the same transitions by the end of the year.[165] Changes had not yet been authorized for Pemaquid, and as it turned out, changing actual lighthouses over to automated systems would take a bit longer than anticipated—longer than simply adding an automated buoy might take.

Community representatives from Bristol wrote to the lighthouse service, or specifically to their U.S. representative, about the matter. Representative Edward C. Moran Jr. then wrote to the commissioner of lighthouses.

Pemaquid Point Lighthouse

Above: The sun sets. *Photo by Trudy Irene Scee.*

Left: Inside the bell room is an anchor and other items to look at. *Photo by Trudy Irene Scee.*

At the end of July 1934, the question was answered. Moran sent the following telegram: "Commissioner Lighthouses advises Pemaquid Point Light to be retained, power increased and made flashing with establishment of gong buoy to replace fog signal. Station to be unwatched." So, the major questions were resolved—the light tower would be retained but not the lightkeeper.[166] But some questions remained.

In late September, the *Lincoln County News* reported that just a few days before, "Pemaquid Light was abandoned by Capt. Roy Elwell Tuesday and the light changed over to an unattended flashing light." No longer would the "rugged reef" have a "human eye to scan the water and send help to those in trouble as has so often been done in the past. Again machinery has supplanted man and only electrically controlled signals will warn those who need a guiding and assisting hand hereafter." Thereafter, a gong buoy—painted red and located about 1,170 yards from the tower in thirty-six-foot deep water—would replace the fog bell, which had sounded every ten seconds in foggy weather. The light would flash every ten seconds—a two-second flash followed by an eight-second dark period. The candlepower would be increased to 1,300 candela and electricity would be introduced to power the new system.[167]

The lighting apparatus eventually installed at Pemaquid, and at many lights, was a four-bulb lamp changer, which rotates bulbs as one burns out, immediately replacing it with another. Bulbs were specially made 250-watt ones. The lamp changer was installed inside the Fresnel lens. In addition, although the bulbs generally used regular hard-wired electrical sources, at Pemaquid, a set of batteries was installed at the base of the tower with a switch so that in the event of a power failure, the light would still have power. Further automation and innovation have since reached Pemaquid Point.[168]

The questions about land ownership had not yet been resolved with the transition to automation, though. The *Lincoln County News* in 1934 advocated that the property should forever remain open to the "sons and daughters of the state and to the tourists who visit this wonderful coastal region, [some] of whom linger to make their homes in the county."[169] The question would not be answered for a few years, and apparently, some people who owned land nearby were also concerned that were the point to become privately owned, they would no longer have access to the ocean, albeit access limited by the cliff and rocks.

The United States Coast Guard took control of the light at Pemaquid, as of other American lights, in 1939. Pemaquid is now part of the Boothbay Harbor Coast Guard Station and the larger First Coast Guard District. The

Pemaquid Point Lighthouse

Above: And the light changes. *Photo by Trudy Irene Scee.*

Opposite: Another view from the top of the tower. *Photo by Trudy Irene Scee.*

Pemaquid Point Lighthouse

district extends from the Canadian border to New Hampshire's southern border and is one of twelve in the United States.

On the eve of the changeover, on May 7, 1939, Robert Thayer Sterling wrote an article for the Maine press announcing that the 150th anniversary of the Lighthouse Service would be celebrated in all the lighthouse districts in the United States. The week of August 7 had been scheduled for that purpose, and Thayer mentioned Pemaquid in his discussion of the Maine lights. A small photograph of the light was included with the story.

In "150th Year of Lighthouse Service to be Observed This Summer," Sterling, a lighthouse fan of many years, noted that Maine had been "very lucky in having so many lighthouses." Moreover, the coast as a whole had seen many improvements in recent years, such that "during the past few years there have been many lights put out of commission and sold because the new modern devices in lighting equipment has brought this about. Where lights were operated by keepers they are now unattended through new inventions." During this week in August, light stations would open to the public, so they might see how they operate, including close examinations of the lighting apparatus. The U.S. Postal Service was in the process of creating a stamp to commemorate the 150th anniversary of Pemaquid Point and Monhegan lights, both noted as being built during the early nineteenth century. Sterling stated that

"Hundreds of people visit these stations each year. There is only one station where a keeper is still in charge and that is Monhegan. Pemaquid is now unattended and only a custodian is employed."

In a caption for a small photo of the light at Pemaquid, Sterling noted that Pemaquid, "next to Portland Head, probably receives the largest number of visitors each year." The year before, some three thousand people had registered to enter the tower at the Portland Head Light, while perhaps as many others had visited but not entered the tower.

Sterling also published a book about Maine lighthouses in 1935. Although the section devoted to Pemaquid is quite brief, Sterling attested to the popularity of the Muscongus Bay light, stating, "This light has always figured as one of outstanding lighthouses on the Maine coast and has possibly been photographed as often as any outside of Portland Head." He stated, too, that Pemaquid "has figured prominently ever since it first showed its beam of light to mariners on the Atlantic."[170] Almost two centuries after its installation, its popularity had only grown, even with the changes in lighthouse administration.

In his coverage of the light at Pemaquid in his *Lighthouses of the Maine Coast and the Men Who Keep Them,* Sterling did lament the loss of the men who had manned the light for decades: "The handshake of the keeper has gone and the summer vacationist greatly misses the greeting that he always looked forward to for so many years. The fog signal station here has been discontinued, and the light station changed to an unattended one. Mr. Roy Elwell who has entertained many thousands of summer tourists during his many years as keeper has retired to another station much different than the one he has left behind."[171]

Sterling wrote soon after the last keeper left, and he personally felt the loss of someone who had been a close acquaintance, if not a friend. Leroy S. Elwell had moved to the Spring Point Ledge light near Portland, which was indeed a different sort of light and in a different environment. At least for a time, Pemaquid's last lightkeeper had found a new station.

In May 1941, C.L. Knight discussed lighthouse bells and their fate after automation. He noted, "After the change and automation, especially automation, a full-time keeper was no longer needed, although this change was not necessarily viewed as a positive development by everyone."[172]

Nor was the dismantling of the old fog bells welcomed by everyone, as some people had emotional and aesthetic ties to the sound of the old bells and missed hearing them ring out in foul weather. As Robert Thayer Sterling wrote in 1939, "With the going of the lighthouses goes the parting sound of the bells." Many were then piled up at the wharf at the Lighthouse Depot in South Portland.[173]

While the public and lighthouse personnel adjusted to the new situation, the town of Bristol had already decided to lease the property and use it as a park. It had passed its first hurtles and established its park while talks with the government continued. The town soon entered negotiations with the federal government to establish a more permanent situation, eventually entering a contract to buy the land, except for the tower itself and a small piece of land around it about thirty-five feet square, to allow the government continued access for maintenance and other needs.

In 1939, the same year the Lighthouse Service was integrated into the U.S. Coast Guard, President Franklin Delano Roosevelt signed a bill authorizing the federal government to convey "unused portions" of the land around the tower to the town for a park. The U.S. government and the Town of Bristol subsequently signed a deed to the land in September 1940. The Coast Guard maintained control of the tower and light. The town made the balance of site into "Lighthouse Park," something it had already initiated. A local artist group added a gallery in 1960, and a formal museum would later be added in the keeper's house. The station was identified as number 287.

According to some documents, the town agreed to pay half of the appraised $4,300 value of the property, amounting to $2,150, payable annually with an interest rate of 2.5 percent. However, according to lighthouse websites, the town ultimately paid $1,639. At the time of the sale, the light was still being fueled by gas. William Sawyer—the man whose body would later wash up near the lighthouse—served as the caretaker of the park and the lighthouse.[174]

As it had done at other locations, the Coast Guard soon removed the old fog bell from the premises, much to the disappointment of some people at Pemaquid. The Coast Guard no longer needed the old bell there after the fog system was automated. The Coast Guard would later donate a smaller replica bell to the museum, which now hangs on the bell house. A larger bell, more like the one that hung in the top position on the bell house, is currently situated on the lawn.[175]

There is a small fee for entry to the park and the various buildings. Against the wishes of at least some locals, in May 2000, the Coast Guard licensed the tower to the American Lighthouse Foundation. The arrangement has seemed to work out well. The Friends of the Pemaquid Point Lighthouse (a chapter of the American Lighthouse Foundation) maintains a space on the ground floor of the tower, and its docents are available to answer questions

Pemaquid Point Lighthouse

The keeper's house at Pemaquid Point is now the Fisherman's Museum. *Photo by Trudy Irene Scee.*

and educate people about the tower, the lantern room and other aspects of the lighthouse.[176]

The tower itself is open to visitors at scheduled times during the summer season, and on those days, one can climb the stairs to see the Fresnel lens. It is a difficult climb in some ways but worth undertaking if you are able to do so. You can look at the lens in the lantern room, understand what that scuttle is at the top of the ladder that awaits the climber where the staircase ends and look out over the ocean, rocks and grounds below.

Next door, in the keeper's house, the Fisherman's Museum holds a number of items of interest to the historian and the general visitor. The museum was set up by the townspeople of Bristol and opened in 1972. Volunteer docents and others maintain the museum. It holds gear and artifacts related to Maine fishing and to the light, as well as model boats, a collection of photographs and various albums related to the region, fishing and Pemaquid Point.

One of the two most-noted items on display is a large ship binnacle—a ship's compass and its enclosure. The enclosure, or binnacle, protects the compass, and sometimes other instruments, from sea spray and from falling over from the constant rolling and pitching of a vessel, even in relatively calm weather. The one on display is especially marvelous, as it is made of

Pemaquid Point Lighthouse

Right: The tower is now staffed by Friends of the Pemaquid Point Lighthouse, although the Coast Guard still has control of the light and fog systems. *Photo by Trudy Irene Scee.*

Below: Those who wish to see the inside of the tower enter through the door visible to the right of the tower. The door to the Fisherman's Museum is perpendicular to it. *Photo by Trudy Irene Scee.*

brass and wood and in excellent condition. Another notable item in the museum is a fourth order Fresnel lens like the one in the tower, which was secured from the Baker's Island light by the Coast Guard. This is a truly invaluable addition to the museum, as it allows the many people who are unable to climb the spiral staircase—there are posted requirements meant to protect the public—to see an actual workable lens and understand a bit about how a lighthouse light actually works. Again, volunteer staff is happy to answer questions.

The upstairs quarters of the keeper's house at Pemaquid Point is available for rent and rumored by some to be haunted. According to staff, the apparition is a woman wearing a red shawl and seen most often resting by the fireplace. The ghost is purportedly wet and shivering. Some suggest that she may have been one of the people lost at sea near the point or someone waiting for a loved one to come back from sea. People have also reported hearing unexplained noises, such as doors slamming, as well as lights going on and off in the upstairs rooms for no logical reason.

In 1991, an April storm damaged the bell house and tower significantly, and later that same year, Hurricane Bob caused further destruction. The following year, the bell house and tower were restored. The bell house is open to the public in the summer, and many people look inside to see an old ship anchor, as well as a few other items of interest.

Bordering the lighthouse property and the park, descendants of the Martin family—the family who sold the land to the government to establish the lighthouse in 1827—opened a restaurant and gift shop in the 1900s, after automation at the light. Guy and Myra Martin opened the business on family land but sold it later in the century.[177] It remains popular with the seasonal visitors, located as it is just over the fence from the lighthouse. A number of older hotels continue to provide lodging to visitors, some of which have done so for a long time.

Public interest in the light has never waned, nor have the dangers presented by the rugged coast at Pemaquid decreased. Drowning and maritime mishaps continued from the 1930s through today. Including a few examples here may suffice to illustrate some of the recent history of the location and to warn the visitor that this is indeed a wonderful place but that one needs to take care when navigating the Maine waters in the Pemaquid area and to stand back much farther than what might at first glance seem necessary when visiting the lighthouse and neighboring properties.

Long after the last official keeper and the despondent caretaker had turned off the light in the dwelling house and locked the door in 1934 and 1942,

Pemaquid Point Lighthouse

The Christmas and holiday season was white in 2018–19, as more snow fell after this photo was taken. The fence is decorated with wreaths to mark the season. *Photo by Trudy Irene Scee.*

The keeper's house. *Photo by Trudy Irene Scee.*

respectively, on Sunday, October 24, 1965, the *Mary Ann*, a 180-foot modified sardine carrier launched in 1948 from Thomaston and owned by the Holmes Sardine Packing Company, went aground near, but not at, Pemaquid Point, on Thrumcap Island. The Coast Guard rescued the captain, Elliott Wotton of nearby Friendship, responding to his Mayday calls. Wotton was alone on the boat, and his Coast Guard rescuer, Lee Court, rowed through five- to seven-foot waves to reach the stranded boat, according to the *Rockland Courier Gazette*. The boat had a destroyed keel and bottom, and the Coast Guard gave up attempts to free it shortly after 4:00 p.m. on Sunday. A tugboat sent to it likewise gave up its salvage mission. Wotton was only the second person to captain the ship—the first having been George Hicks, who had launched the boat almost two decades previously.[178]

Tragically, rescue attempts were not as successful with the life of one woman in 1982. On August 10, Karen Simmons of Fort Plain, New York, was on vacation with her family in Maine when her two children were swept off the rocks at Pemaquid Point by a rogue wave. She and her husband jumped into the water to save the children, ages twelve and thirteen. Someone on shore threw a life ring out to the family, according to a Coast Guard spokesperson. Hauntingly reminiscent of the 1903 shipwrecks, those on shore were able to pull in the two children and the husband, but when it was Karen Simmons's turn, the line broke, and she drowned before the eyes of those on shore. A Coast Guard boat soon reached her, but it was too late.[179]

In 2011, a male artist visiting the region narrowly escaped drowning after his backpack was swept off the rocks. He decided to go in after it. He quickly pulled on his swimming trunks and entered the ocean just east of the lighthouse and the nearby Sea Gull Shop. Bristol Fire and Rescue responded and was about to launch a water rescue, when after struggling for about fifteen minutes, starting before the rescue personnel arrived, the man was able to pull himself out. He was exhausted and lucky to get out alive, according to the Bristol fire chief. He had entered the ocean from the precarious rocks of Pemaquid and got into the undertow. He was taken to a hospital for evaluation.[180]

In 2014, a report of a boat in distress off the point came in, but searchers did not locate the one sighted, and it seems that it made a narrow escape or was possibly a hoax. In 2015, a father and son were swept off the point by a high wave, and then in January 2016, in the chill of winter, a Maine woman climbed out on the rocks to get a better look at the ocean following a storm. One of Pemaquid's infamous—to those who know the point—rogue waves knocked her off the rocks and into the sea. The woman's husband was with

Pemaquid Point Lighthouse

Above: An aerial view of the tower and the park. *U.S. Coast Guard photo.*

Left: A drawing of the 2003 Maine State quarter featuring the Pemaquid Point Lighthouse. *Public Domain.*

her, and there were other people present as well—Pemaquid is a popular place even during and just after winter storms. The woman was able to get out of the water, as were the man and his son after some struggle. Luckily, those times, there were no deaths.

The Bristol fire chief spent some time after the 2016 accident warning people to back away from the rocks below the light. As he described it, "They were on the west side of the rock, which allowed her not to be pulled back into the ocean." As the chief further warned, the waves at Pemaquid might be fine—not too rough—for a good five to ten minutes, and then a larger wave could come in, as it did in this instance. The woman was taken to the hospital from the Pemaquid Lighthouse.[181]

Pemaquid Point Lighthouse

An actual uncirculated Maine State quarter from 2003. *Photo by Trudy Irene Scee.*

The waves at Pemaquid are not all the same size, and this has been a danger for centuries. Other drowning and near drownings have occurred, just as other boats have had problems off the coast, even as larger shipping vessels have largely disappeared from the area in recent decades, as commerce in America and the world has changed.

In 2003, the citizens of Maine chose the Pemaquid Point Lighthouse to be on its new state quarter. Also on the quarter is an engraving meant to resemble the schooner *Victory Chimes*—the last three-masted member of the Windjammer Fleet. Gulls circle above the ocean, and although the tower is exaggerated in size compared to those of the keeper's house and other buildings, it is clearly the Pemaquid Point light on the Maine state quarter.

On the Maine quarter, as in reality, the lighthouse continued to look in good order, but by the early 2000s, extensive damage was apparent from water seeping in through deteriorating mortar. Grants were secured from the National Trust for Historic Preservation and from the Maine Historic Preservation Commission. The Friends of Pemaquid Point Lighthouse raised the remaining funds, and a major restoration project was soon underway. Based on recommendations by Building Conservation Associates (BCA), the exterior coating of the tower was removed along with the deteriorating mortar, and the tower was repointed and repainted.

Memorial plaques have been erected at Pemaquid Point Lighthouse and in the area to honor those who came to its dangerous shores in the 1600s. Descendants of the *Angel Gabriel* shipwreck survivors from 1635 have participated in the various dedication ceremonies. Those at the light were mounted on rocks on the far side—the one away from the ocean—of the lighthouse and commemorate the survivors in general and the families of survivors Ralph Blaisdell and John Cogswell in particular. These families donated the bronze memorial plagues.

In addition, in August 2010, descendants of *Angel Gabriel* survivor William Furber and others held a dedication ceremony for a memorial plaque at the Colonial Pemaquid Archaeological site, where research and excavations had continued since the turn of the twentieth century. Furber had come to

Pemaquid Point Lighthouse

The keeper's house in winter 2017. *Photo by Trudy Irene Scee.*

Left: The Fresnel lens on display in the Fisherman's Museum. Kept lighted, it gives the viewer an appreciation for how the lighthouses work. *Photo by Trudy Irene Scee.*

Below: Buoys and other items on display at the Fisherman's Museum. *Photo by Trudy Irene Scee.*

Above: Tools of Maine's fishing industry and its history are available for public perusal, and education. Visiting the museum also lets the visitor see what an actual keeper's house may have looked like. *Photo by Trudy Irene Scee.*

Right: In almost total darkness the light in the tower does not illuminate the ground around the lighthouse, although it shines its beacon out to sea. There are lights mounted along the building but not many. *Photo by Trudy Irene Scee.*

Pemaquid Point Lighthouse

Up the stairs, through the doorway and up the inside staircase. Some say you might see an apparition here. *Photo by Trudy Irene Scee.*

Pemaquid Point Lighthouse

Right: The keeper's house in winter. *Photo by Trudy Irene Scee.*

Below: The carriage house at the Hotel Pemaquid. *Photo by Trudy Irene Scee.*

Pemaquid Point Lighthouse

Darkness descends. *Photo by Trudy Irene Scee.*

Pemaquid Point Lighthouse

the region as an indentured servant to the Cogswell family. He earned his freedom in the New World in a few years and subsequently ran a ferry in what would become New Hampshire.[182]

The now-automated lantern of the Pemaquid Point Lighthouse still shines a white beam seventy-nine feet above mean sea level every six seconds. The beam is currently strong enough to reach fourteen nautical miles out to sea in ideal weather conditions, and it is fully automated, switching on and off at dusk and dawn.[183]

Not far away, Pemaquid's sister lights shine out warnings. The Monhegan Light to the southeast flashes every thirty seconds, the Ram Island Light to the west casts a steady red beam, the Cuckolds Light to the south of Cape Newagen "with group flashing every six seconds" and a white fixed beam radiates from Sequin Island. Mariners in the area are well warned, and the lights to the northeast and southwest send their warnings as boats approach or leave the area. Those who are uncertain as to which light is which can consult the Coast Guard Light List, although GPS instruments now provide immense aid to mariners.

Pemaquid Point Lighthouse was listed on the National Register of Historic Places in 1985. It is one of almost sixty lights in Maine still in operation—one well-worth visiting.

CONCLUSION

Lighthouses are generally unmanned today. Automation means that a timer or computer can turn the lights on at dusk and turn them off at dawn. They can be activated from afar in inclement weather. Foghorns, likewise, can be set to go off when necessary.

Larger ships generally do not need lighthouses any longer. Radar and their own automation systems guide them through treacherous water, darkness and fog. Foghorns and bells would not even be heard in larger ships with their layers of enclosures.

Moreover, the large sailing and steam ships used to transport Maine and other Canada Maritimes ice, lumber, fish, paving stones, coal and other cargos have largely disappeared. Ocean cargo does still arrive in America, but the routes are generally different, while cargo that would have gone via the coastline has largely shifted to inland trucks, with some railroad and air competition. The world of 2020 is not the world of 1820.

Smaller boats still use lighthouses as navigational aids, as do fishing boats, and Maine has many of both. And, just as importantly, the lights have a significant place in national and state history, and they have entered the hearts of the public.

Go to Pemaquid on any nice day at any time of the year, and you will find people there—people amazed at the rocks and the cliffs and the roar of the ocean, aiming cameras up to the tower at dusk or dawn, waiting to try to catch the light in their own lens as it revolves into the sky. Go in bad weather, and you are still likely to find a few people there. But if you go often, you will find those moments alone when it is just you and the cliffs and the water and the tower that has sent its guidance out to mariners for almost two hundred years. There is peace at Pemaquid but dangers too. Look out for rogue waves, do not fall over a cliff or stumble too close to the point—it could be your death. Do not try to bring a small boat too close to the shore—that, too, could prove fatal.

And still, in spite of the danger, the light is magic. Just remember, it was put there for a reason.

Appendix

PEMAQUID POINT LIGHTHOUSE KEEPERS

NAME	DATE OF APPOINTMENT
1. Isaac Dunham	November 3, 1827–37
2. Nathaniel Gamage (or Gammage) Jr.	June 13, 1837–41
3. Jeremiah Mears (or Means)	1841–45
4. Ephraim Tibbets	1845–49
5. Robert Curtis	July 31, 1849–53
6. Samuel C. Tibbetts	April 9, 1853–58
7. John Fossett	February 12, 1858–61
8. Joseph Lawler	March 29, 1861–69
9. Marcus A. Hanna	July 30, 1869–73
10. William A. Sartell	July 31, 1873–83
11. Charles A. Dolliver	September 28, 1883–99
12. Clarence E. Marr	August 16, 1899–1922
13. Herbert Robinson	1922–circa 1928
14. Leroy S. Elwell	circa 1928–34

Assistants to the Keeper, or Temporary Keepers
Rufus McKinney Jr.	circa 1898
Herbert E. Brewer	circa 1898–99

NOTES

Chapter 1

1. Holland, *American Lighthouses*. The individual lights generally have basics of their histories covered on their own websites. Some have individual books.
2. Ibid.; see Davidson, *Lighthouses of New England* for general information, although in most instances, Holland has more detail and specifics. Also see records of the U.S. Coast Guard for this and following information. The friends of the individual lighthouses and local organizations also have basic information on their websites and literature.
3. Holland, *American Lighthouses*. This covers the growth of lights under Pleasonton.
4. Specific Friends of a given lighthouse will have this information.
5. Holland, *American Lighthouses*. Also see F. Ross Holland, *Lighthouses* (New York: Metrobooks, 1995. This is the same person, using different publication names. See Holland for much of the following information. Although other sources contain some of the same information, Holland's fist work is the most inclusive, and it seems the source for some of the other authors.
6. See later chapters on this.
7. Holland, *American Lighthouses*.
8. Ibid.

9. General sources.
10. General sources for lighthouses during the era.
11. Ibid.
12. Ibid.
13. General sources for the era; *Cobblestone Magazine*, June 1981. This work for youth included a clear explanation of the lenses, as well as a number of interesting articles for young people.

Chapter 2

14. Cartland, *Twenty Years at Pemaquid*; general sources.
15. "History of Pemaquid Point," Fisherman's Museum; Libby, "Guide to Pemaquid Lighthouse."
16. General sources; Libby, "Story of Pemaquid Point."
17. Libby, "Story of Pemaquid Point."
18. Ibid.
19. Ibid.
20. Ibid; surviving note from Isaac Dunham.
21. Holland, *Lighthouses*.
22. General sources for Pemaquid Point.
23. Libby, "Story of Pemaquid Point."
24. Ibid.
25. "New England Lighthouses, A Virtual Guide"; general sources for the remainder.
26. "New England Lighthouses, A Virtual Guide."
27. *Lincoln County News*, November 21, 1984; general sources on presidential involvement.
28. Wheeler, "History of the Administration." The I.W.P. Lewis Report is reproduced in part.
29. Ibid.
30. U.S. Documents for Pemaquid Point, Untitled Documents. Documents currently on file at Pemaquid Point.
31. *U.S. Department of Commerce and Labor*.
32. U.S. Documents for Pemaquid Point, Untitled Document.
33. Lighthouse record on file at Pemaquid Point, with general sources on the tower; Libby, "Story of Pemaquid Point."
34. Libby, "Story of Pemaquid Point"; general sources.
35. *U.S. Department of Commerce and Labor*.

36. Tag, "Lighthouse Lamps Through Time." This includes the general use of acetylene gas. Little is known about its use specifically at Pemaquid Point, but it was introduced in 1934 if not sooner.

Chapter 3

37. From general sources on American lighthouses and based on conditions and events at Pemaquid Point, as are following paragraphs unless otherwise indicated.
38. Cartland, *Twenty Years at Pemaquid*.
39. Assembled from records on file at Pemaquid Point.
40. Federal Lighthouse Service records.
41. Assembled from records on file at Pemaquid Point.
42. Ibid.
43. Ibid.
44. Ibid.
45. Assembled from various general sources.
46. "Minot's Ledge Lighthouse," Lighthouse Friends.
47. Ibid; Snow, *Famous Lighthouses of New England*.
48. General sources; Cartland, *Twenty Years at Pemaquid*.
49. Snow, *Famous Lighthouses of New England*.
50. Ibid.
51. The author has been unable to find further information related to Fossett, even through federal record searches and perusal of other Maine lights. Perhaps Fossett did not find being a keeper to his liking and/or soon moved on to other pursuits. All keepers do not necessarily show up in searches, though.
52. U.S. Coast Guard records; Bachelder, *Shipwrecks and Maritime Disasters*; Salata, "Keeper at Cape Elizabeth;" and "Coast Guard Tender Named for Bristol Man," October 23, 1997, clipping on file at Pemaquid Point.
53. U.S. Coast Guard records; Bachelder, *Shipwrecks and Maritime Disasters*; Salata, "Keeper at Cape Elizabeth;" and "Coast Guard Tender Named for Bristol Man," October 23, 1997, clipping on file at Pemaquid Point.
54. U.S. Coast Guard records; Bachelder, *Shipwrecks and Maritime Disasters*; Salata, "Keeper at Cape Elizabeth;" and "Coast Guard Tender Named for Bristol Man," October 23, 1997, clipping on file at Pemaquid Point.
55. U.S. Coast Guard records; Bachelder, *Shipwrecks and Maritime Disasters*; Salata, "Keeper at Cape Elizabeth;" and "Coast Guard Tender Named for Bristol Man," October 23, 1997, clipping on file at Pemaquid Point.

56. U.S. Coast Guard records; Bachelder, *Shipwrecks and Maritime Disasters*.
57. Federal Lighthouse Service records.
58. National Archives, "Lighthouse Keepers and Lifesaving Personnel in Selected Entries."
59. General sources; "Coast Guard Tender."
60. National Archives, "Lighthouse Keepers."
61. Snow, *Famous Lighthouses of New England*.
62. *Official Register of the United States*, Volume 1, circa 1873.
63. U.S. Department of the Interior, *United States Register Containing a List of Persons Employed*.
64. Wheeler, "Keepers New Clothes."
65. Ibid.
66. Small, *Lighthouse Keeper's Wife*.
67. Ibid.
68. See U.S. Lighthouse Service records for these moves and individual light records.
69. Clayton, "Lighthouse Marrs."
70. Assembled from various sources, as are following paragraphs unless otherwise indicated. Records and publications of the Fisherman's Museum and Friends of Pemaquid Point; Libby, "Story of Pemaquid Point."
71. Cuckholds Lighthouse. Salary information comes from federal government records. Sources have Elson at two different lights during the era.
72. Small, *Lighthouse Keeper's Wife*.
73. Singer, "Tragedies and Near Tragedies."
74. Ibid.
75. Taken from several general sources. The couple may have had more than one daughter, as more than one name has been found for a daughter.
76. Singer, "Tragedies and Near Tragedies."
77. D' Entremont, "History of Petit Manan."
78. Small, *Lighthouse Keeper's Wife*.
79. From an article stamped August 15, 1927, from "Just Talks," on file at the Maine State Library.
80. Singer, "Tragedies and Near Tragedies."

Chapter 4

81. Specifics on the ship provided by the Department of Agriculture, Conservation and Forestry. The balance is from general sources.

82. General sources for Pemaquid Point.
83. Ibid; Mather, "Journal of Richard Mather"; Snow, *Great Storms and Famous Shipwrecks*.
84. Mather, "Journal of Richard Mather."
85. Ibid.
86. Snow, *Great Storms and Famous Shipwrecks*; general sources on the storm.
87. Snow, *Great Storms and Famous Shipwrecks*.
88. Small, *Lighthouse Keeper's Wife*.
89. *Bath Daily Times*, September 17, 1903.
90. From record on file at Pemaquid Point Lighthouse and local press. See next three notes.
91. *Bath Daily Times*, May 5, 1891.
92. Ibid., May 6, 1891.
93. *Bar Harbor Record*, May 7, 1891.
94. *Bath Daily Times*, May 6, 1891.
95. Ibid.
96. Ibid.
97. Ibid.
98. Ibid., May 7, 1891.
99. Ibid., May 11, 1891.
100. Keeper's report from 1893, available at Pemaquid Point.
101. Cartland, *Twenty Years at Pemaquid*.
102. Ibid.
103. Ibid.
104. Report on file at Pemaquid Point.
105. Ibid; *Portland Sunday Telegram*, November 3, 1940.
106. *Bath Daily Times*, May 11, 1891.
107. General sources, in particular, local newspapers, previous work by the author; Cartland, *Twenty Years at Pemaquid*.
108. Cartland, *Twenty Years at Pemaquid*.
109. *Bath Daily Times*, November 28, 1898.
110. Ibid.
111. Ibid., November 29, 1898, and subsequent days.
112. Ibid., and subsequent days.
113. Ibid., November 30, 1898.
114. Ibid., December 6, 1898.
115. Ibid.
116. Ibid.
117. *Bangor Daily Commercial*, September 18, 1903.

118. *Bangor Daily News*, September 18, 1903.
119. *Bangor Daily Commercial*, September 25, 1903; report from Pemaquid; *Bangor Daily News*, September 18, 1903.
120. *Bangor Daily News*, September 18, 1903.
121. Ibid.
122. Ibid.
123. Report of September 17–18, 1903. Possibly reprinted in the *Boston Journal*, September 18, 1903. Transcribed copy on file at Pemaquid Point Lighthouse.
124. Ibid.
125. Ibid.
126. Ibid.
127. *Bath Daily Times*, September 17, 1903.
128. Ibid.
129. Ibid.
130. *Portland Herald*, September 18 and 19, 1903.
131. *Bangor Daily News*, September 18 and 19, 1903.
132. Ibid., September 18, 1903.
133. Ibid., September 17, 1903.
134. Ibid.
135. Ibid.
136. Ibid.
137. Ibid., September 19, 1903.
138. Ibid.
139. Ibid.
140. Ibid.
141. Ibid.
142. Boothbay report of September 23; *Bath Daily Times*, September 23 and 24, 1903; Town of Bristol Annual Report for 1904 on file at Pemaquid Light.
143. Singer, "Tragedies and Near Tragedies"; general newspaper sources.
144. Singer, "Tragedies and Near Tragedies"; general newspaper sources.
145. Cartland, *Twenty Years at Pemaquid*; Snow, *Famous Lighthouses of New England*.
146. *Bangor Daily News*, September 19, 1903.
147. Singer, "Tragedies and Near Tragedies." No date of the event is given, but this has been reported elsewhere.
148. General sources; Labrie, *Story of Pemaquid Light*.
149. *Bath Daily Times*, August 17, 1917.
150. Ibid.
151. "Pemaquid Point Lighthouse, Maine," Lighthouse Friends.

152. October 11, 1930 news release from the U.S. secretary of commerce, as reprinted in the *Springfield Republican*, October 15, 1930.
153. Ibid.
154. Ibid.
155. Ibid.
156. *Bath Daily Times*, September 18, 1945.
157. *Bangor Daily News*, September 17, 1945.
158. Ibid.
159. Ibid.
160. *Bath Daily Times*, September 18, 1945.
161. Ibid.
162. Ibid.
163. Ibid.; *Bangor Daily News*, September 18, 1945.
164. *Bangor Daily News*, September 19 and 20, 1945.

Chapter 5

165. *Bath Commercial*, May 9, 1933; *Bangor Daily Commercial*, May 9, 1933. Portland release on file at Maine State Library.
166. *Portland Press Herald*, July 31, 1934, reprinted.
167. *Lincoln County Herald*, September 28, 1934.
168. General sources; Labrie, *Story of Pemaquid Light*.
169. *Lincoln County Herald*, September 28, 1934.
170. Sterling, *Lighthouses of the Maine Coast*.
171. Ibid.
172. Knight, May 3, 1941.
173. Sterling, "Fog Bells."
174. Federal documents and Pemaquid Point Lighthouse internet sites.
175. The Fishermen's Museum. thefishermensmuseum.org.
176. This and following information taken from Pemaquid Point Lighthouse internet sites and from author's personal observation over many trips to the lighthouse.
177. Labrie, *Story of Pemaquid Light*.
178. *Rockland Currier Gazette*, October 26, 1965.
179. Article retrieved from a Fort Plain, New York article posted on findagrave.com. Look for newspapers in Maine.
180. *Lincoln County News*, June 30, 2011.

181. *Bangor Daily News*, January 17, 2014; *Lincoln County News*, January 26, 2016; *Bangor Daily News*, January 26, 2016.
182. *Lincoln County News*, August 12, 1910.
183. General sources for Pemaquid Point, with information on "lantern" from Fisherman's Museum publications.

BIBLIOGRAPHY

Bachelder, Peter D. *Shipwrecks and Maritime Disasters of the Maine Coast*. Portland, ME: Provincial Press, 1997.
Cartland, J. Henry. *Twenty Years at Pemaquid, Sketches of Its History and Remains*. Pemaquid Beach, ME: Maine Moore, 1914.
Cobblestone Magazine. June 1981.
Clayton, Richard. "The Lighthouse Marrs of Maine." *Lighthouse Digest Magazine*, September 2008.
Davidson, Donald W. *Lighthouses of New England From the Maritimes to Montauk*. Edison, NJ: Wellfleet Press, 1990.
D'Entremont, Jeremy. "History of Petit Manan Lighthouse, Near Corea, Maine." New England Lighthouses: A Virtual Guide.
Find a Grave. findagrave.com.
"The History of Cuckolds Light Station. https://innatcuckoldslighthouse.com.
"History of Pemaquid Point." Fishermen's Museum. September 10, 2014. https://www.thefishermensmuseum.org/history-of-the-pemaquid-point-light.
Holland, Francis Ross, Jr. *American Lighthouses, Their Illustrated History Since 1716*. Brattleboro, VT: Stephen Greene Press, 1972.
"Just Talks." August 15, 1927. Maine State Library.
Knight, C.L. Article dated May 3, 1941, on file at the Maine State Library.
Labrie, Rose. *The Story of Pemaquid Light, a History of Pemaquid Point Installation*. Hampton, NH: Hampton Publishing Company, 1961.

BIBLIOGRAPHY

Libby, Hilda. "The Story of Pemaquid Point Lighthouse." On file at the Maine State Library, Augusta, and the University of Maine, Orono. 1975.

———. "Guide to Pemaquid Lighthouse." Museum pamphlet.

"Lighthouse Keepers and Lifesaving Personnel in Selected Entries." National Archives.

Mather, Richard. "Journal of Richard Mather." *Chronicles of Massachusetts*, 1846.

"Minot's Ledge Lighthouse." Lighthouse Friends. Lighthousefriends.com.

New England Lighthouses, A Virtual Guide. Jeremy D'Entremont. http://www.newenglandlighthouses.net.

Official Register of the United States Volume 1. 1873.

"Pemaquid Point Lighthouse, Maine." Lighthouse Friends. lighthousefriends.com.

Records and publications of the Fisherman's Museum and Friends of Pemaquid Point.

Salata, Nick. "Keeper at Cape Elizabeth Two Lights Answers the Call." *Lighthouse Digest*, 2003.

Singer, G.W. "Tragedies and Near Tragedies of Pemaquid Point Light." *Lewiston Journal*, February 2, 1924.

Small, Connie Scovill. *The Lighthouse Keeper's Wife*. 1986. Reprinted with introduction by Andrea Constantine Hawkes. Orono, University of Maine Press, 1999.

Snow, Edward Rowe. *Famous Lighthouses of New England*. Boston: Boston Printing Company, 1945.

———. *Great Storms and Famous Shipwrecks of the New England Coast*. Boston: Yankee Publishing Company, 1943.

Sterling, Robert Thayer. "Fog Bells from Discontinued Lighthouses on Maine Coast Lay Silently on Cape Wharf." February 18 and 19, 1939. On file at Maine State Library.

———. *Lighthouses of the Maine Coast and the Men Who Keep Them*. Brattleboro, VT: Stephen Daye Press, 1935.

Tag, Thomas. "Lighthouse Lamps Through Time." United States Lighthouse Society. https://uslhs.org/lighthouse-lamps-through-time.

Town of Bristol Annual Report 1904. On file at Pemaquid Light.

U.S. Coast Guard records, various years and publications.

U.S. Department of Commerce and Labor. *Lighthouse Service, Atlantic Coast of the United States, List of Buoys and Other Aids to Navigation, Maine and New Hampshire, First Lighthouse District*. 1911.

Bibliography

U.S. Department of the Interior. *The United States Register Containing a List of Persons Employed*. Undated, late 1800s.

U.S. Documents for Pemaquid Point, Maine, Untitled Documents for "Pemaquid Point Light-Station, Me." 1856–99, unless otherwise noted. Documents on file at Pemaquid Point.

U.S. Lighthouse Service records.

U.S. Secretary of Commerce news release. October 11, 1930.

Wheeler, Wayne. "The History of the Administration of the USLH Service." *Keeper's Log*. November 2014.

———. "The Keepers New Clothes." *Keeper's Log*. November 2014.

Newspapers

Bangor Daily Commercial
Bangor Daily News
Bath Daily Times
Boston Journal, 1903
Lewiston Journal
Lincoln County News
Lincoln County Herald, September 28, 1934
Lincoln County News
Portland Sunday Telegram, November 3, 1940, report from Bristol
Portland Press Herald
Rockland Currier Gazette, October 26, 1965

ABOUT THE AUTHOR

Pemaquid Point Lighthouse is historian and photographer Trudy Irene Scee's seventeenth book and a labor of love, written for her brother. While Scee writes for the general public, she also holds undergraduate degrees in forestry and history, a master of arts in history from the University of Montana and a doctorate of philosophy in history from the University of Maine. She has received a number of academic fellowships and awards and taught history at Mount Allison University in New Brunswick, the University of Maine and Husson University in Bangor. She now works with disadvantaged and other youth part time, while working full time as an author.

Dr. Scee has published a number of books on Maine history and culture, as well as on other subjects. She has also held photographic exhibits and worked as a journalist. Her other books published by The History Press include *City on the Penobscot: A Comprehensive History of Bangor, Maine*; *Tragedy in the North Woods: The Murders James Hicks*; and *Mount Hope Cemetery of Bangor, Maine: The Complete History*. Additional works are underway. Dr. Scee lives in Maine.

Visit us at
www.historypress.com

www.ingramcontent.com/pod-product-compliance
Lightning Source LLC
Chambersburg PA
CBHW042140160426
43201CB00021B/2348